#10
Wilmington Branch Library
1300 N. Avalon Boulevard
Wilmington, CA 90744

SIMPLE IS THE NEW SMART

10

SIMPLE IS THE NEW SMART

26 Success Strategies to
Build Confidence, Inspire
Yourself, and Reach
Your Ultimate Potential

Rob Fazio, PhD

Foreword by Neil Cavuto

158.734
F287

SEP 28 2016

226641034

CAREER PRESS

Copyright © 2016 by Rob Fazio

All rights reserved under the Pan-American and International Copyright Conventions. This book may not be reproduced, in whole or in part, in any form or by any means electronic or mechanical, including photocopying, recording, or by any information storage and retrieval system now known or hereafter invented, without written permission from the publisher, The Career Press.

SIMPLE IS THE NEW SMART
EDITED BY ROGER SHEETY
TYPESET BY PERFECTYPE, NASHVILLE, TN
Cover design by Howard Grossman/12E Design
Cover image by Auris/iStock
Printed in the U.S.A.

To order this title, please call toll-free 1-800-CAREER-1 (NJ and Canada: 201-848-0310) to order using VISA or MasterCard, or for further information on books from Career Press.

The Career Press, Inc.
12 Parish Drive
Wayne, NJ 07470
www.careerpress.com

Library of Congress Cataloging-in-Publication Data

CIP Data Available Upon Request.

DEDICATION

To Dad.
If you were around today, you'd be the second
person in line to buy a copy.
The first person would be the one that got ahead
because you were kind enough to Hold the Door.
Thank you. *143*

ACKNOWLEDEGMENTS

The simple part I got, the smart part, I needed a lot of help with. Saying this book wouldn't be possible without the years of dedication and hard work of my sister Lauren Fazio in an awesome understatement. Thank you for balancing my love for rhymes and acronyms with your love for detail and accuracy. Also, thank you to my favorite communications professor and loving wife, Dr. Keli Fazio, a woman who has a gift for being so honest with so much heart. This book wouldn't have been possible without my in-laws Geri and Dave Steuber ßfor being supportive, patient, and providing a little wine along the way.

Thank you to my literary agent, Leticia Gomez for her expertise, counsel, and focus. Jackie Klee, I appreciate the years of inspiration, encouragement, and gentle and genuine reminders get the book done. Thank you to my friends Cathy Swody (Thrive Leadership), Sacha Lindekens, Jeff Graddy, John Gates, and Steve Williams (Avion Consulting), for furthering my thinking and supporting my drive for all things practical, positive, and simple. I'd also like to thank Todd Alexander for his consistent mentoring and confidence in my path. Thank you to Maritza Caro-O'Donnell for her positive energy, and willingness to help me throw my passion into the book, while making it practical.

To the clients that continue to work with me, thank you. You drive me to learn and be ready for the range of challenges that we find solutions for. Becca Goldstein, although we didn't find all the answers we were looking for on our first trip to that literary workshop at UPenn, we eventually got it! Thanks for the smarts and smiles as I wrote this with your support.

Thank you to the most well read man I know, JP Mantey, for his willingness to follow his passion and to help others in the process. A special thank you to the rising star, Cait McNair for her research, insights, and eagerness to excel.

I am consistently inspired by the enthusiasm, warmth, and positive energy of Joy and Lee Zaben, it kept me focused on writing the right stuff. Thanks to my long time buddy Mike VanBuskirk for showing me what priorities and resilience are all about.

And finally a thanks to my mom, "Janet," who has likely already proudly promoted this book more than any marketing firm could ever do. Dreams do come true!

CONTENTS

Section 3: Leading

Section 4: Accelerating

FOREWORD

Like Father, Like Son

From Opening Doors to Opening Minds: Lessons from Rob Fazio

Of all the tragic stories of September 11, 2001, perhaps none hit home or hit my gut quite like that of one Ronald Fazio. When the first plane hit the first tower, Ron was on the 99th floor of the South Tower and chose to lead the charge and hold the door for others scrambling out from that building.

They survived. Ron did not. But that one selfless courageous act inspired a nonprofit in his honor, appropriately named "Hold the Door for Others." For Ron's son Rob, it was his way of not only recognizing his father's heroic act, but making something good out of such a senseless tragedy.

Without fail, for as long as I've covered the 9/11 anniversaries, I've always sought out Rob to put perspective on the day unlike any other. I don't think I've ever finished a single interview with a dry eye or without a lump in my throat. With warmth and even good humor, Rob would recount his father's meaningful life, down to his love of Reese's Peanut Butter Cups. Apparently, the story goes that when Rob and his family were waiting out the long and torturous days for any news on their dad, they'd leave his favorite snack on posters and leaflets to urge him home. They wrote on his flyer, "If found, please feed Reese's Peanut Butter Cups." He never returned, but to this day, Ronald Fazio's engraved name at the old South Tower site often includes a Peanut Butter Cup atop it. Nothing stops me more in my tracks than that simple act of love—a poignant and sweet reminder of a robust and bigger-than-life soul lost forever.

I once asked Rob if the anniversaries ever get easier, or whether seeing the terrorists' planes hitting those buildings, and their subsequent collapse, ever gets to be too much. Although we all lose loved ones, rarely is their passing—their murder—cued up each year for the world to see, again and again. He shrugged his shoulders and simply said, "I don't see it that way. I see it as a way to remember and share my dad."

Frankly, I don't know how he and his family stay so composed or so focused. Then I stepped back to see that was Rob. That was his family. That was their collective DNA. It was and is as if they're all genetically wired *not* to whine, complain, or make excuses. So they would hold their grief and focus on the lasting image of a dad holding a door.

That's where this uplifting and actionable book on success comes in. It's sort of like "Hold the Door 2.0." Or maybe I should say, "Hold the Door—times 26." Because unlike the selfless single act of one individual that inspired a foundation, this book details 26 key strategies that take that undertaking to a whole new—and varied—level. And who better to write it than a guy like Rob, who has walked the talk, and lived and grown to tell about it. It's that perspective gained through pain that painfully reminds us all: life is short, so maybe we should go long. Maybe in our personal lives and our professional lives we should stop making excuses and start making a lasting difference.

Rather than succumb to the personal and professional issues that can often hold us back, Rob reminds us they are the stuff of which character is made and, ultimately, how a life is defined and many a successful career is built. I like the way Rob characterizes his approach: "We will all fail. If you fail, I want you to fail forward and see a failure as feedback, a moment, not a permanent barrier."

Though we may not all experience the severe trauma of so public and devastating a personal loss as Rob and so many other 9/11 families experienced, as this learned psychologist and executive adviser has aptly pointed out, we share the same emotional hits that sadly can define humanity. We all lose or feel loss. We all stumble or see others stumble. We all know what it's liked to be passed over, or passed by. We all know what it's like to be out of sorts and sometimes sort of out of hope.

Rob guides us not with lectures, but with love; not by dwelling on the issues that bedevil us, but those that teach us, guide us, and that form our own tower of strength. That's Rob's greatest gift here—building a nonprofit that is stronger than any buildings and more meaningful than any bad day's disruptions.

The more I read, the more I marveled at how a guy who lost so much could forgive so much, overcome so much, and teach us so much that can be applied to business and life. It's easy for someone who has lived a charmed life to think he can guide less charmed lives. It's quite another coming from someone who has not, and yet has learned so much more. From pain comes passion. From disaster comes deliberation. From senseless loss comes lasting love.

In all my years covering the greatest success stories in the corporate and political world, I've come to find that those who truly stand out are the ones who keep dusting themselves off so they *can* stand up. Most have been disarmingly kind, even humble—very focused, but very fun and often *funny*.

That's Rob to a tee: a man who, like his dad, appreciates the ride of life and not the bumps in that ride. He learns from the bumps and helps us learn as well—it's what guides the truly successful among us in how they interact. And it's no act. To play off a line Rob uses, their character is their currency. And their currency is invaluable, because their passion for excellence and decency is invaluable as well.

What's more, Rob keeps it simple and focused. Maybe because he's concluded that life is actually pretty simple as well. Seeing through the oddities and cross-currents of everyday living, it's the little things that matter—like sticking to your word, sticking to a schedule, and sticking to your guns. That's what's so simple here and so smart. It's a page-turner *because* it turns us back to the basics—the stuff that matters, the discipline that matters, the spirit that matters, the very essence of a productive life that matters. This isn't a book about simply opening doors; it's a primer on not closing off opportunities. It's about conquering our inner doubts and demons, and rising to something more—much more.

I like to think of it as Rob's way of saying life is like a big cup, and one defined by what we pour into it. Enjoy every gulp. Every moment. No matter the cup, no matter what's in the cup. Just like Reese's—it's something to be savored and enjoyed.

Short and sweet. But lasting. Very lasting. Very . . . satisfying.

Neil Cavuto
Fox Business Network and Fox News Channel

INTRODUCTION

People want to see progress. I always wondered what all the chatter was regarding Dyson and their line of cleaning products. Why would anyone pay more for a "dust buster" that was really loud and then talk about it as if they had just won something? Then I used one. The difference isn't just the technology and ability to clean; the difference is that they give you a view into your progress. They let you see the mess that you clean. There is a see-through plastic canister that gives you insight into what you have accomplished. I never thought I would think this, but I actually get a sense of accomplishment from vacuuming and I'm ready to do some more. What's my point? When we see progress, we feel progress. When we feel progress, that gives us confidence and motivation and we move forward fast.

This is a book about success. It's not about just anyone's success; it's about your success. There are several obstacles to success. Trust me; I used to be best friends with the biggest obstacle to achieving success, myself. Part of my shift came from learning that if you can be successful, then you can help others be successful and that fueled my fire. I can't promise you that all of your dreams will come true. I can promise you that if you read this book with an open mind and challenge yourself to apply what you learn, then you will increase your probability of success and decrease your probability of distress.

Walk past any large bookstore window, log on to Amazon or Barnes and Noble, and what do you see? Hundreds, if not thousands, of book titles that are created with one reason in mind: to get you to buy them. What makes this book different? This book is one that I would buy because its focus is simple. It's about taking the *smart* cuts, not just shortcuts, to get you long-term gains. I have struggled my whole life to integrate information in the way that society determined it was supposed to be integrated. Reading comprehension was never my thing, so I needed to find a new way, a simpler and smarter way, for me to get ahead. I did and I want to share it with you.

I can remember being in 6th grade and everyone in the class needed to do a book report. I hated book reports. I got so intimidated because it was hard for me to remember as I read. I would lose the key points and not be able to integrate and recall all of the information in the format that the teacher asked for. One day, the teacher said that we could choose to do a verbal book report. Rather than following the written template, we could do a presentation on the book in our own way. Considering I figured it couldn't get worse than what I had been doing, I gave it a shot.

Because I knew that I wasn't going to be able to remember all aspects of the book, I prioritized on what I knew the teacher always asked about. She wanted to know about the key people, the plot, and the "so what." Therefore, I worked backward. I read the back of the book, the last few pages, and the first page of each chapter. It gave me what I needed to do the verbal book report. I took a smart cut that gave the teacher what she wanted and I actually learned and remembered more about that book than any other. Keep in mind, I am not just suggesting taking shortcuts; I advocate for smart cuts, which are intentional and based on weighing the costs and benefits. I do believe that people misinterpret time and struggle for value and impact. If you can do something in half the time and get twice the return, wouldn't that be of interest?

Why is Simple the New Smart?

Twice the gain, half the strain is the foundation for *Simple Is the New Smart.* Success in work and life will never be easy, but it can be simple. For some reason we make our work and home life more complicated than they need to be. It has something to do with the way our minds work, and we are constantly looking for something to hold on to or to move toward. In my experience as a psychologist, I have always been shocked at how many people need to worry about something or find something that challenges them beyond what they can actually handle. Too often, people get caught up in their own complexity. Clear thinking and concise communication are currency, especially when interacting with intelligent and powerful people.

My point is that if you are intentional and strategic about how you approach your work and life goals, you can get there faster and directly. It takes discipline and the ability to move through disappointment fast so you can move forward faster. We will all fail. If you fail, I want you to fail forward and see a failure as feedback, a moment, not a permanent barrier.

Simple Is the New Smart Standards

Standards set the bar and guide behavior toward a direction. Let me be crystal clear. The following standards will give you freedom within a framework. Use these principles as a guide to empower you to pursue your definition of success.

Where You Put Your Focus First is Where You Will Finish First

Intention is the steering wheel for success. Contrary to popular books or pop psychology blogs, simply stating where you want to go will not get you there. It can certainly help, but you also need focus, prioritization, strategy, and execution. By putting your focus on the right things first, you will be setting the right direction. What I mean by this is that you want to focus on what brings you closest to your success first. It's about prioritization, not preference. If you want to get in shape, you need to make working out the right way a priority and do that before other things get in the way of distracting you from your goal.

Move In, Move Out, Move Forward

One of the best simple strategies is effectively dealing with feeling. If you run away from it or avoid it, you will pay for it with interest later. If you stay stuck in it, you can't move forward. The best strategy is to let yourself feel what you feel and then move forward. You can always come back to the feeling. As a matter of fact, I encourage people to face their feelings head on and literally schedule time to confront what they are feeling so they don't get blindsided. A basic example of this is someone who goes through a breakup that they didn't want. If you just simply keep busy and avoid it, eventually it will hit you or infiltrate your next relationships. What's better is have a combination of keeping yourself busy and distracted, as well as carving out some time to deal with and explore what you feel.

I was asked to go on NBC in New York City just after the Newtown, CT shootings. That situation was horrible and sad. One of my key recommendations to people dealing with trauma is to not take the adage "time heals all wounds" at face value. My belief is that it's not just time that heals wounds; it's what you do with time that heals wounds. My point here is that there are healthy ways to deal with tough situations and intense feelings. If you challenge yourself to move in (deal with what you feel and honor your experience), move out (allow yourself some distractions and relief), and move forward (continue to grow and focus on the future), you will be more likely to heal in a healthy way and focus on the future while honoring your loss or adversity.

Fit, Fight, or Flight

In the beginning of the book, I mention the work of Dr. Bob Sternberg on *Successful Intelligence* (Sternberg, 1997). Much of his work, as well as meeting with him, has inspired my thinking through the years. One of the core concepts Dr. Sternberg has written about is a person's ability to be successful in an environment, or to change the environment, or, if that's not possible, find a new environment. I believe this has a direct link to working within a culture. I simplify this as fit, fight, or flight. If something is a fit, great, stick with it and go for it. If something isn't a fit, you need to decide whether you can influence the situation and make the needed change (fight). If not, it may be time to go: time to go to a different role or a different organization (flight). Knowing what is realistic and what you can and can't do is critical to your success. If you can't be successful in what you want to be, you need to make a move forward. That move could be to influence change or that move could be to just plain move.

Success isn't Easy, but it is Simple

The premise of this book is to help you take a direct path toward success through applying simple strategies that work. The best strategies are the ones that you apply. There are a host of claims out there stating that people forget up to 90 percent of what's exposed to them. However, other people claim that is not true. What I can tell you is that in my work with people, whether it is reviewing with them what we learned a month ago or a year ago, people are busy and they do not internalize and remember things unless they have some key factors. Though I'd like to believe that advisers, coaches, and consultants change the world for the better, the truth for me lies in that there are some key factors that determine whether something sticks and can become a positive habit.

There are three factors I have learned that make a simple strategy effective, sustainable, and most likely to be used in the real world. A strategy that is simple and successful is appetizing, digestible, and memorable. Strategies that people apply need to be something they want (appetite), easy to understand and apply (digestible), and easy to recall (memorable). Throughout this book, I aspire to deliver to you approaches that you want, that you can understand, and that you can remember. That's my recipe for a simple strategy. The reason I believe it works is that when I talk to people days or years later after a training or coaching engagement, the things they are still leveraging to succeed are the ones that follow this formula. I think of it as what people want in a good meal: something that is appetizing, digestible, and memorable.

I focus on topics that seem either to be a challenge by most or needed by most, hence there is an appetite and a desire to learn. Simple strategies that can be easily understood, recalled, and applied are the ones that matter. I want you to be able to use them in a moment's notice.

The reason I focus on simple strategies is that people are under constant pressure and need to be able to call upon strategies that are simple to remember and simple to apply.

Lead or Deal

If you aren't willing to lead, then you will have to do the opposite, deal. This doesn't mean that you always have to be in charge, or be the boss, but it does mean that you need to take action toward your success. When people lead it means they care enough to move toward something, rather than dealing with something. Another creative way to think about this is on my desk every day of my life. Dr. Jim Burke gave me a graduation gift. It was a paperweight, and one that I love to this day. It says, "If you're not the lead dog, the view never changes!" Now I'm not suggesting you always need to be the alpha personality, but what I am saying is that we all need to find opportunities to set a direction, or the direction will be set for us.

See it, Say it, Start it

My basic premise for development and learning new skills is taking intentional action. Everyone learns in different ways. I am a visual person who needs to be able to see something to learn something. I recently got married and my wife and I had the "brilliant" idea of taking dance lessons. During the first few weeks, I could not remember a single move. Then I started to bring index cards to the lessons. I needed to find my way to see it, say it, and start it. *See it* is about creating an image of what I'm learning. I drew and visualized my version of the moves. I created my own graphic that made sense to me. *Say it* is about being able to communicate what I learned in a concise and simple manner. I changed the names of the dance moves into my own language that I could remember and that made sense to me. Often, I use acronyms, words that rhyme, or words that all start with the same letter. Then comes *start it*, which is all about action and creating positive habits. This is when I got out of my own way and just tried and applied. I focused on what I knew and what made sense to me. What's my point? Had I not had a process to learn the dance moves, I would have gotten nowhere and kept getting frustrated. Don't get me wrong, I am still a terrible dancer, but my wife and I had a blast and nailed our first dance.

How to Get the Best out of This Book

As I stated earlier, when I grew up I wasn't a traditional student. I didn't read a lot and I didn't comprehend as quickly as others. I knew I needed a different way to excel. I learned through people, experiences, and conversations. In fact, if I am being completely honest, the only reason I got into and through my doctorate was learning from failures, leveraging experiences, and relying on relationships. I'm not saying I'm proud of my struggle and challenges, but I am saying I know there is more than one way to succeed. Always respect what you don't have and always leverage what you have.

This book is designed to help you learn and apply what you want and forget the rest, until you want it or need it. *Simple Is the New Smart* is a choice. It was written with the reader in mind; not just every reader, but the reader who wants to get ahead. You will see each chapter has a setback and a simple strategy. Many of the chapters will also include a "sound bite." A sound bite is something that is simple and memorable that has impact in a concise manner.

I learned the art of the sound bite from a close friend, Vicki Elkins, who was advising me on speaking with authority. She taught me a valuable equation for the first time I was on live television. Being that she was an expert in public relations and communication, she knew a formula that worked. She taught me that $Q = A + 1$. What this means is that a **Q**uestion = an **A**nswer plus **1** statement you want to make. Essentially, whatever you are asked, give your answer and add your point of view. The other valuable lesson I got related to media was from KLIF radio host Grant Stinchfield, who is a former NBC reporter. He taught me the art of talking in sound bites. His advice was to speak in a concise manner that is memorable. What's my point in talking about media? What works on live TV works in real life. People need to receive information that is memorable and easy to apply.

The way to get ahead is to choose your own pathway. To use a term from some of the only childhood books I gave some time to, this book is a choose-your-own adventure. By my own admission, I am a chapter and book jumper. Find what interests you or what you need to develop or strengthen and go for it. Read the Introduction and then look through the table of contents and choose your own adventure based on what setbacks you want to address or areas in which you want to excel. My advice is to come back early and often to this book so you can continue to excel. I never was and never will be a traditional learner, so this book isn't written in a traditional way. Set your own path and learn your way. I can't promise you that this book will be the most scientific or a best-seller, but I can promise you that it comes from a person who cares about helping you help yourself succeed. The more simple strategies you learn, the faster you will blow past your potential and perform. Although there are 26 strategies (which may seem like a lot), the simplicity is in your selection and prioritization.

Factors Based on the Psychology of Success

Hard work is just not good enough to get ahead anymore in life and business. If you don't believe me, think of the people around you who work a lot harder than you, but achieve less. It could be the executive who over-analyzes everything, works nights and weekends, and never seems to get caught up. It could be a person who has their own business and doesn't understand the importance of leveraging others and not doing everything themselves. I see it every day and it's a shame. As you progress in your life and career, you have less energy and more to do. Soft work becomes more important than hard work. This is the case for working with intention and becoming a master of simplicity on your road to success.

It starts with working with intention. If you work with intention, you can actually *take it easy* and become successful with fewer barriers. When you are intentional, you have focus and are not distracted by all the noise the world around you presents. We all need to leverage what comes naturally and what we enjoy. Granted, it takes time and hard work to find out what you are good at, and to have the confidence to choose the easy way out. An example of this is someone who is gifted at analytics. The tendency is to move them into a different role and help them develop, when, in reality, the best thing for them and the organization is for them to flourish at analytics. What typically happens is the painful process of trying to change the person rather than focusing on fit.

There are countless theories and everyone has an opinion. The one that I believe counts the most (aside from your own beliefs) is that of Dr. Bob Sternberg. He introduced an aspect of intelligence that is often not an area of focus. He created the concept of *successful intelligence* (Sternberg, 1997). Successful intelligence includes three areas:

→ **Analytical:** to solve problems and to judge the quality of ideas.
→ **Creative:** to formulate good problems and ideas in the first place.
→ **Practical:** to use the ideas and their analysis in an effective way in one's everyday life.

Dr. Sternberg's work has given legitimacy to what is important in everyone's life—success. That is, knowing what you want and developing the skills to get there or adapting. His work will serve as a platform for the simple strategies taught throughout this book.

This book is designed with success in mind while keeping the pursuit simple. That means I will teach what works. We have all learned myths about how people learn and develop. Many of these myths, such as simply "putting your intention out to the universe" not only do not work, but I believe cause more frustration and anxiety than growth.

The Four Foundations of Simple Is the New Smart

Based on my experiences and research, I have come up with the Four Foundations for Success: *Psychological Swagger, Reading, Leading,* and *Accelerating.* Seeing and saying what you want to do will help, but staying positive, knowing your setbacks and strengths, building the skills and "how to," and holding yourself accountable are just as critical. These Four Foundations for Success capture each of these key components.

1. **Section 1 (Chapters 1–6):** *Psychological Swagger.* Psychological Swagger is the starting point for how you feel, think, and act. It creates the synergy between belief and behavior. What you believe sets the tone for your success or failure, and determines how "mentally secure" you are. It is the difference between winning and losing. The best athletes get this and so can you. For the most part, when an athlete gets to the professional level, his or her physical talent is on the same level, but the mental toughness is what separates those

who excel from those who stay average. There is great power in believing in yourself, having grit, and creating a positive vibe. Dr. Steve Danish, the founder of the Life Skills Center at Virginia Commonwealth University, told me, "I want you to find the confidence to match your abilities." He was absolutely right, and confidence is a big part of Psychological Swagger.

2. **Section 2 (Chapters 7–13):** *Reading.* What do you choose to hear about yourself, your performance, and your potential? How we listen, most often selectively, creates awareness, which is essentially what you know about yourself and your situation. It includes a continuous effort to learn, and the fact that there are things you don't know. Awareness is critical to success because what you don't know can hurt you. Often, people end up somewhere they don't want to be because they had a blind spot from only listening to those things they wanted to hear.

3. **Section 3 (Chapters 14–20):** *Leading.* Thinking fast is a critical skill for success, and one that is both natural and can be taught. Thinking fast is working smarter, and the third key to taking the "easy" way out. Having the capability and skills to work your plan is all about increasing your competence, which in turn increases your confidence. There is something called *deliberate learning.* It comes

from the work of Ericsson, Krampe, and Tesch-Romer (1993). They found that when people intentionally focus on learning something, their brains actually create pathways that will help focus on that development. Remember the last time you heard a word for the first time and then you heard it again and again? That's because you made your mind aware and it began searching for that word. In other words, you brought it into your consciousness. The same is true for committing to building ability. Train your brain and you will see progress.

4. **Section 4 (Chapters 21–26):** *Accelerating.* Momentum is one of the hidden secrets of success, and the key to momentum is perpetual—and purposeful—forward motion. Accountability is about two things, holding yourself accountable and maintaining forward progress. It's not just about catching yourself when you aren't staying the course; it's also about an attitude adjustment to get you back in the game.

These Four Foundations for Success serve as a platform for your movement toward success. In any goal or dream you deem worth pursuing, you need first to build your foundation.

When I was in college, I took a class in exercise science. We studied the impact of different types of workout routines and the impact it has. I can remember a conversation with someone who said that he knew about how the athletes trained. He said that Penn State football players only do one set per weight lifting exercise. This went against everything I had learned, so I asked why. I'll never forget what he said: "Because if a Penn State football player can do a second set, they didn't do the first one right." This means that if they were physically able to do another set within a certain period of time, they didn't put their maximum effort into the exercise. Wow, talk about building a foundation for mental and physical strength. Let me be clear, I have no expertise in how these football players trained, but I can tell you that story had an impact on me. It gave me a little bit of Psychological Swagger and I became more focused on building my foundation for success.

Let's get to the first simple strategy and begin to build.

Section 1

Psychological Swagger

1

Insecurity
Install a Security System

*If you think you can or you think
you can't, you're right.*

—Henry Ford

I t all starts with attitude, which is the foundation for
Psychological Swagger. There are countless quotes and
motivational stories related to the importance of attitude. Quite simply, it is the differentiator between those
who complain and those who train. Everyone faces challenges in their pursuit of success, but few have the grit to
stay the course and maintain their focus. A core aspect
of attitude is belief, your belief in yourself as well as your

belief in how the world works. The lens through which you see things takes you either toward your success or away from it.

We all have insecurities. Those of us who use them can lose them. Insecurities can limit our progress in life. An example of this is letting a thought about the past predict your future. For me, a major insecurity was my lack of "traditional intelligence." I always struggled with standardized tests and getting good grades. Earlier in life, this was what I focused on because it's what most people valued and where emphasis was placed. With time, I made my insecurity my greatest strength.

A story I heard years ago illustrates this point rather well. A husband and a wife were driving along the highway and the husband was complaining about the windshield being dirty. He pulled off to a rest stop and asked a gas station attendant to clean the windshield. After the windshield was cleaned, the man started complaining about the incompetence in the world and how the windshield was still dirty and all he could see was dirt and blurriness. When the husband was done with his rant, his wife leaned over and took off her husband's glasses and asked, "How do you see things now?" To the man's surprise, everything was crystal clear. It wasn't the windshield that was dirty, it was his glasses. This little story is a great illustration of how the lens through which we see things impacts our experience.

A successful person I'd like to introduce you to is Roland Trombley, Senior Vice President and General Manager at Comcast Spotlight. I knew Roland was an illustration of how attitude leads to success within the first moments of speaking to him. The following is the simple success strategy that Roland recommends.

Roland Trombley is the inspiration behind "Power Seller" at Comcast Spotlight. "Power Seller" is an innovative sales strategy that tailors roles to talent. This strategy frees "all stars" up from administrative tasks and allows people to leverage their natural skill sets that drive revenue. Roland has been a true transformational leader. Many people have visions for cultural change and increasing organizational effectiveness, but very few are successful. Roland was successful by leveraging his simple strategy of building confidence within people.

His philosophy is that the biggest success comes from people who believe in their ability. When people are willing to travel outside their comfort zone, they push themselves and others to learn and grow. The initiation of a strategy at the top is irrelevant if the middle managers aren't equipped and confident to execute.

Roland explains that it's all about motivating people through confidence. A key to creating that confidence is as simple as communication. However, one-to-one communication alone is not sufficient. It is about creating a culture and system of communication. He believes in creating plans for communication on a weekly basis throughout the year. The discipline of being upfront and transparent builds credibility and respect. This motivates people and creates alignment.

Insecurity can be fuel for confidence. Many executives lead without paying attention to what people need in order to feel more confident and comfortable. This is especially critical in times of change when pressure arises and people fold back into their comfort zones. Confidence is what makes comfort zones larger and helps people to make decisions and act intentionally rather than reactively.

A quote that stands out from the conversation with Roland is, "The reason I am successful is because I worked for a horrible boss!" During this experience, Roland learned how a leader could be a detractor of performance rather than an enhancer of talent.

Roland's advice is to find opportunities to build your confidence and grow confidence in others and "own it." There are many ways to build confidence within yourself. One is to identify a skill that you want to master. Commit to that skill by reading about it, watching videos, and finding people you trust to provide honest feedback. Building confidence in others is a combination of caring and challenging. This means demonstrating support for the person and continuing to challenge them to grow by giving them stretch assignments. If it's in a professional setting, or even if it's outside a professional setting, it's about encouraging the person to grow by doing things outside their comfort zone.

We'll all face insecurity with our careers. The way to counteract insecurity is to have a foundation of confidence, and the best way to do that is to install a security system.

Simple Success Strategy: Install a Security System

Early on in my career, I let my insecurity of not being "smart" fuel my passion and desire. I began to learn about other types of smart. I researched the impact of emotional intelligence and developing people smarts. This is not to say that traditional intelligence doesn't matter. It does, but I have found that other aspects of life lead to a much more productive and successful career and life. I shifted my focus to what I can do, rather than what I didn't believe I could do.

I saw the author of *Blink* (2007), Malcolm Gladwell, speak about the differences between cultures and how when American children are confronted with a difficult math problem, they say to themselves, "I don't know how to do this." However, when children in areas of Asia are faced with the same situation, they say to themselves, "I haven't found the solution yet." This connected to me because it is the difference between how I used to live my life and how I live it now. When I was a kid in school, anytime I saw that little asterisk that told you the homework question was more difficult, I immediately shut down and thought to myself that I wasn't going to be able to solve the problem.

With time, I reframed the situation and used it to leverage my strength, connecting to people and building relationships. I began asking for help from those who naturally were able to solve those difficult problems. The result changed my life. People were willing to help and I developed deeper connections by using my vulnerability as a strength.

As years passed, I replaced my insecurity of not being smart with the confidence that I can find a way to learn. I realized that I learned best through conversations and interactions with people. It has been a driving force for me and has paid tremendous dividends. It has become a differentiating strength in that when I teach someone something, it is in simple terms; because if I understand it, most people will. I am not shy about talking about where I struggle. In fact, I offer that without hesitation.

We can all do this. We can find what insecurities limit us and develop confidence to break through these limitations. This has a positive snowball impact. We all have insecurities that surface, most of which we are not even aware. The shift from insecurity to security and confidence has a ripple effect.

What insecurity has been a part of your life? How can you shift this to a security and become confident? Our minds work like computers; they operate according to how we program them. The more we can develop positive programs, the more you will get positive outcomes. A very practical and effective way to counteract insecurity is to build yourself a foundation of security. This security system serves two purposes: 1) it consistently builds your confidence and 2) it buffers the impact of experiences that may test your confidence.

The way the security system is built is through positive self-statements and building your *confidence corral.* These statements are strong and positive about yourself. The following are examples of these statements. Take five minutes to create five more.

Self-statements:

1. I am confident.
2. I believe in myself.
3. I bounce back from adversity.
4. I am strong.
5. I focus on what I can control.

There are a few guidelines in order for the self-statements to work:

1. All statements must be positive and about you.
2. You have to believe 100 percent in the statement.
3. Say the statement like you mean it, with feeling.

To start, say these statements to yourself every night for one month. Then you can shift to three times a week. My clients have taught me that it is helpful to have them on an index card or have a Post-it reminder on their bathroom mirror.

The more you tell yourself that you believe in yourself, the more it will become the norm that you will take on challenges. Personally, I went from being fearful of what I wasn't able to do, to passionate about learning and excelling. With time, I built up what I call my *confidence corral*. My confidence corral is all of the things that bring out my confidence. It can be things I say to myself, what I wear, who I talk with, the way I stand, what I eat, or the questions I ask myself. It's just like a pre-shot routine that an elite athlete goes through. The more I make confidence a norm, the less chance insecurity gets to create a storm.

2

Doubt

Put Doubts in Your Doubts

Our doubts are traitors, and make us lose the good we oft might win, by fearing to attempt.
—William Shakespeare

F azio, why did you quit?"

I remember the day like it was yesterday. I was sitting in my high school auditorium. I was overweight, pushing 215 as a sophomore; a sophomore full of doubt, insecurities, failures, fears, and lists of what I couldn't do. Behind me, the voice of the best athlete in our high school, and the starting varsity quarterback, belted out the words: "Fazio, why did you quit?" It was the loudest thing I have ever heard and something I never want to hear again.

I loved sports and loved playing them. I was good at sports, not great, but good, and better than most at a few things. However, I was consumed with worry and fear about what people thought instead of what I felt and thought. This misdirected focus kept me from succeeding.

My worry and doubt started early for me. When I was young, I played baseball. Every minute of every game, all I worried about was what would happen if the ball were hit to me. It made no sense, because when the ball came to me, I knew what to do and did the right thing. I would traumatize myself with each pitch. I was so scared that I would literally wet my pants with every pitch. I know this sounds a bit crass, but I need you to know what it was like for me to be stuck because of my doubts. My parents had to ask special permission for the umpire to let me be the only one on the field to keep their uniform untucked.

How did I get to the quitting? As a freshman, I was too afraid to go out for the football team because I was just too scared. I knew I could play and be good, but it was something new and I was afraid. I didn't play football freshman year, or any sport for that matter. All I did was wish I were playing. I felt like a loser and, in many ways, I was a loser. At the start of the next year, I decided to try out for football. I lasted less than a week. Every practice, all I said to myself was I was too far behind and couldn't do it. I hated every minute of it and quit. I defeated myself. That's why the quarterback called me out.

Then one day in gym class midyear, Coach Fred McClain pulled me off to the side and said, "Come see me after school, you are going to throw shot put." I was scared to death, but he saw something in me, or he saw something on me—most likely my huge gut and rather large chest and shoulders. I threw shot put that year, and I gained some confidence. Finally, senior year, I made a simple decision. I went out for football again. I wasn't great, but I did it and fought through my fears. It was the start of my path to learning that no matter how many doubts I had in myself, there was always a voice inside of me that knew I could. I made a choice to focus on what I could do rather than what I knew I couldn't do. I know this seems simple, but it changed my life and that grit stuck with me, and I leverage it every day.

Now I don't hesitate to get up to play or get the ball any time and every time. Of course I get nervous, but I own it and use it. I still fail all the time, but I fail forward. I went from being a kid that wet his pants at the thought of a baseball being hit to him, to someone who thrives at the opportunity to be on live TV and talk to the nation about how to be your best when things are at their worst. I share this not to be arrogant or to brag, but to illustrate the power of going from doubt to confidence. Trust me, if I can make the shift, so can you.

There's not much worse in life than being a slave to your doubt. Doubt is just as bad, if not worse, than hearing from others that you can't do something. Doubt is something internal. It's a feeling, an association, and a recipe for failure. I can remember working with an executive who reeked of doubt. He was someone who was intelligent and well established, but riddled with doubt. He hesitated with every decision and every move. The doubts led to indecision and eventually ate away at his confidence and, worse, his competence. The challenge is that doubts can get a hold on us and emotionally cripple our progress. The gift is that once you control them, new opportunities arise.

Doubts are emotional beliefs that we create and give power to. You need to analyze your doubts just like you would analyze a business decision. The downside of doubts is an ugly experience. Anytime emotion comes into play it feels like fact. Feelings are not fact; they are just our associations with experiences, but we have a hard time determining what is fact and what is fiction. The truth is that most doubts are fiction that we make into fact. Because our minds follow the direction of our emotions, it is very easy to let doubt consume you.

Simple Strategy: Put a Doubt in Your Doubt

Renowned psychologist to athletes, Dr. Al Petitpas, teaches athletes that in order to be successful, you need to keep your doubts in check. His strategy that I have seen work tremendously is to put doubts in your doubts. I have seen him turn people's level of performance in sport and life around with this strategy.

In some of my early work with elite athletes, I put this simple strategy into practice. I was consulting a diver who was talented and successful. He had won many events and was on the way to dominate an event a second year in a row. When he approached a national event, he became doubtful to the point that he was unable to perform even in practice. Obviously, this became a huge concern to him, his coach, and his teammates. What didn't make sense was that he had performed daily and year after year, so why in the world would he not be on top of his game? In a word, doubt.

The diver, let's call him Barry, became overwhelmed with doubt. We had to explore what was driving it. It was actually quite simple. It came down to the questions he kept asking himself, which began with "What if?" What if I don't nail the dive? What if I can't execute? What if I failed? What if I don't win again? Although it seemed completely irrational to those around him, it was pure, full fledged, debilitating doubt to him. He was crippled by it and we needed to do something to put a doubt in his doubt. We followed a formula of success that started similar to most formulas of success, which was one of awareness that leads to action.

Scan for Your Doubts

First things first: uncover anything that can be creeping into your thought process that is keeping you from your focus. Often, this can be something that seems as harmless as a gut feeling about who is watching you or the set up of a situation. In this particular case with Barry, the doubts that surfaced were a fear of failure and an overconcern with what people are thinking while they are watching. Make a list of your doubts so you can use them or lose them. We're leaning toward losing them. Keep in mind that fear has a way of being the strongest doubt.

Understand and Verify

Once you identify what the doubts are, you can begin to explore them by asking yourself some key questions: Where are these doubts coming from? What are the triggers for your doubts? Are these doubts real or are they what you have created? Is there any value in your doubts? An example of a doubt having value would be if you have doubt because you feel unprepared and it's impacting your confidence. This would be useful because it's a cue to prepare more.

Identify What the Doubts are Preventing

In order to move forward and take control of our doubts, we need to have something to move toward. Another way of thinking about this is to know the things that doubts are moving us away from. The way to counteract this is by asking yourself a simple, yet powerful question: "What would I achieve if I didn't have any doubts?" This question gives us forward momentum. Think of this as creating a vision for success that focuses on the positive. The key is to keep this simple, focused, and from a position of strength. The following is an example:

Without doubt, I would take more calculated risks at work. I would be more assertive and give my point of view. I would take more action and expand my responsibilities. I would have laser focus on the three small wins I want to accomplish this year.

Put Doubt in Your Doubts

Next, it's time to shift your doubts through strategic questions. What we're doing here is shifting the "what if" questions to questions that guide us toward our success. Take your list of doubts and answer the following questions similar to the example.

What if . . .

→ I wasn't afraid?
→ I didn't think about what others think?
→ I was confident right now?
→ I was able to get out of my own way?

Shout Out the Doubt

This is where your Psychological Swagger comes in. You need to believe in yourself or no one else will. Belief is contagious. Now take all of your doubts and state them in positive, strong statements similar to the statements in Chapter 1.

→ "I wasn't afraid" becomes: "I know how to manage my fear."
→ "I didn't think about what others think" becomes: "I care more about what I think than what others think of me."
→ "I was confident right now" becomes: "I am confident and strong."

→ "I was able to get out of my own way"
becomes: "Who I am is my strongest asset,
and I help myself win."

Replace the Doubt with Doing

This is where the focus happens and you shift from doubt to doing. Identify one situation where your doubts have held you back, and attack. Leverage your newfound confidence and lean in to your discomfort.

Repeat

Continue to attack your doubts, and before you know it, your comfort zone and confidence will grow, and your doubts will shrink. You will have more power and control over yourself and debilitate your doubts.

Now, I know that all of those steps are great and effective when you have a sport psychologist coaching you through, but what about when you are on your own? Well, it's just like practicing foul shots, nailing a presentation, or perfecting that golf swing. Practice, learn, and practice more. The more positive habits you create, the more ready you will be to deal with doubt.

3

Stubbornness
Releasing Control to Gain Control

You know those people who ask for your advice, but you know that they'll never take it? How about people who, no matter how much they can gain by changing their direction, they just dig their heels in and stay the course? We all know them, and most likely you've been that person at some point in time. It's human nature to want to defend your position and hold your ground, but having the vision to recognize your own stubbornness is a strength. The challenge is to discern between when you're being stubborn because you are right, and when you're being stubborn because you believe you're right.

As I've mentioned a number of times and will continue to do so, emotion is powerful and it can be a constant energizer or energy drainer. When we get stuck in our ways, we run the risk of fighting more for our position just because we came up with it rather than what the best position is. A common trap people fall into is a lack of willingness to give up control in a conversation because you want to win or be right. That's just wrong, and that is the best way to lose perspective, opportunities, and credibility.

A willingness to give something up to gain something is not novel, but it is effective. Think about how many Olympic athletes exchange a normal and relaxing life to make it as an elite competitor. Although I'm not suggesting you become an Olympic athlete, I am suggesting that you can gain a lot by giving up a little. It's all about having a longer-term perspective and being able to see the big picture.

The first step is to see if you may be someone who has a tendency to be stubborn. The benefit of gaining insight into your tendency is you will know what your blind spots are and you will have a chance to make some adjustments if you decide you want to be more open to giving up control.

The good news is that there are some key factors indicating if you have a tendency to hold your ground. Go through the following statements and answer either "yes" or "no" to make a self-assessment of your level of stubbornness.

→ I have a need to be right in most conversations.
→ I prioritize winning more than collaborating.
→ I have a lack of interest in others' points of view.

→ I teach more than I learn.

→ I rarely change my point of view.

→ I know the answer before most people give their points of view.

→ I pride myself on being the first person to give an answer.

→ I talk fast.

→ I prefer to lead a conversation, rather than to listen.

→ If I disagree with someone's point of view, I let them know the first chance I get.

→ More times than not, I try to change other people's points of view.

→ When people tell me what they think, I listen just long enough so I can tell them what I think.

→ I believe that people who change their points of view during a conversation are "flip floppers."

→ When someone disagrees with me, I state my case more forcefully.

The more statements you agree with, the more chance there is that you prefer things your way and it's tough for you to let go. This isn't necessarily a terrible thing. However, I can tell you with confidence that, with time, it will be more and more challenging to partner with people and to motivate them if you don't give them a chance to be part of a decision or conversation. If you have a tendency to be stubborn and hold on to your point of view, the benefit is you will often get your way. The downside is that, with time, people will intentionally get in your way. It's a natural human reaction that if someone is consistently run over and they don't get an opportunity to give their point of view, they will find a way to get their point across, often more covertly than overtly. If you are a boss, your direct reports will be less likely to give you feedback or express their points of view. Just because you have a tendency toward control, doesn't mean you can't control your tendency to control. It's all about versatility.

Simple Success Strategy: Releasing Control to Gain Control

Now that you have a sense of how much control you prefer, let's talk about how you can be better at being versatile and giving up control. It's important to realize that releasing control doesn't mean that you have to completely give up control. The three steps in getting past stubbornness to partnering are *recognize*, *release*, and *revisit*.

Recognize

There are signs that you are not being flexible. You will know from the earlier questions if you have a tendency to want to control conversations. If you do have this tendency, recognizing when you are being overly rigid or getting stuck in your position just because it's your position is an important first step in rectifying the issue. The best way to recognize if you are focusing too much on yourself is to ask one simple question: "Do I understand a point of view other than my own?" If you only know your point of view, there is a good chance you aren't considering the points of view of others. It is okay if you decide that you want to move forward with your point of view and assert your opinion as long as you are aware of the potential consequences. It's about being intentional and weighing the costs and benefits of holding on.

Release

I use the word *release* because if you release something, you can still gain it back. If you release your point of view temporarily, you can still go back to it. When it comes to your point of view, release does not mean lose. The other mistake people make is thinking release means "reload" and coming back stronger with your point.

The way you can release your point of view is to just simply ask some questions. Sometimes it helps people to take a deep breath and focus on listening. A few effective questions to ask yourself are, "Will this matter to the big picture?" or "Is this worth fighting for?" or "What will the impact be if I do or don't stand my ground?" Taking a temporary step back can have a large impact on finding common ground. The more emotionally attached you are to your view, the more challenging it is for you to see the big picture.

Revisit

Once you have temporarily released your point of view, go back to it and see if you still feel strongly. A key strategy is to be able to separate points of view from people. We are all more or less prone to seeing someone else's point of view based on whether we like or admire him or her. Pay attention to your bias and make informed decisions. It is all right to be subjective, as long as you also take the time to be objective.

Success Statements

There are other tools that you can use to help you stay focused on the right things and let go of the unimportant things. One of them is a *success statement*. A success statement is a focused message that guides you. The reason I mention this in this chapter is that there is a difference between being stubborn and being focused. When you are focused, you consider consequences, have grit, and make the decision to move forward. When you are being stubborn, you are getting emotionally stuck and not thinking of the big picture.

You can think of a success statement as a mantra. It's something that you say to yourself that has a positive influence on you and moves you forward. It does not have to be some sophisticated saying or philosophy from a land far away. A mantra is something that keeps you focused on success.

My success statement is: "Fall forward." This is what I say to myself whenever I hit a bump in the road toward my dreams or goals. It tells me to not overthink and to keep moving forward. I know there will be obstacles; I also know that the setbacks are temporary and a positive attitude and mental toughness are stronger than setbacks.

Your success statement should be simple, easy to remember, and have a positive impact on you when you say it.

We all get stuck and we can all be stubborn. My hope is that stuck and stubborn describe where you are, not who you are. Challenge yourself to be flexible and open-minded so you can accomplish more with more people and, of course, if you make a mistake and you fall, fall forward.

4

Helplessness
Become an Owner

It's not if, it's when. At some point we will fall into a victim mentality or see someone else who is stuck in a victim mentality. It happens to everyone and it's normal. The keys are to know the warning signs and to be able to get yourself out of that mindset so you don't make tough situations worse.

Our minds are very powerful and we can either help ourselves by guiding our thoughts or hurt ourselves by letting them go on autopilot. If we don't consistently stay in tune with what our current mentality is, we run the risk of falling into negative thinking, or worse, falling victim to those feelings that we internally, and often inaccurately, turn into facts.

My goal is to help you develop positive habits so you are more likely to convert to an ownership mentality and, if you do fall into a victim mentality, you are able to recognize it and get out of it. I also want you to be able to identify this process in others so you can help them help themselves. This creates a positive cycle of confidence and initiative. Our first step toward an ownership mentality is to learn more about helplessness, which leads to feeling like a victim.

One of the foundational studies in the area of learned helplessness was conducted by Seligman and Maier (Seligman and Maier, 1967). This concept was actually discovered accidently. At first, the researchers observed helpless behaviors in dogs that were conditioned to expect an electrical shock following hearing a tone. The dogs were then placed in a box that had two chambers separated by a barrier that the dogs could walk over. The floor of the box was electrified on one side, but not the other. What happened helped uncover what happens when you lose hope. The dogs that were previously subjected to the electric shock made no attempts to escape even though they could avoid the shock by simply jumping over the low barrier. In other words, they learned that there was no way out.

These findings were very helpful in understanding what happens when we learn that things are outside our control. This is aligned with our previous concepts of focusing too much on listening to negative messages. With time, we learn things that are not necessarily true, but feel like facts. In this case, the dogs learned to lose hope and to feel helpless and defeated because they have no control.

Believing that you don't have any control can be very dangerous, as can only focusing on what you can't control. The key is to know what you have learned incorrectly and not fall into the victim trap. Once you focus on what is happening to you, rather than what you can make happen, you miss out on opportunities and train your mind to give up rather than to have hope.

The Victim Mentality

Although "victim mentality" may sound dramatic, it's a good metaphor for how people frame many of their experiences. Think about how often you say to yourself, "My boss isn't helping me succeed," or "My organization keeps making changes," or "I have too much to do and not enough time." Although this may all be true, it's not helpful to focus all of your energy on these challenges. Too often people focus on what is happening to them and what they can't control, rather than what they can control.

There are many obstacles to keeping motivated and engaged. The setback people fall into is being one of the obstacles by engaging in negative self-talk. There are too many people who already bring us down; we don't need to add to it. How many times in a week do you engage in conversations with others or yourself about what is outside your control? People spend time and energy focusing on what others in the organization think rather than spending their limited time and effort on creating what they want people to do. A positive mental attitude is a key to success regardless of your business, art, or craft. The discipline to remain positive and have focus on what you can do rather than what you can't do yields results. The victim mentality is the enemy of accountability, and accountability is the foundation for productivity. When people fall into a victim mentality they often bring others down with them. This mentality and attitude is contagious.

The Ownership Mentality

Ownership is about getting it done. Someone who has an ownership mentality defines accountability as action rather than blame. Many people in the workplace focus too much on what others should have done rather than on what they can do to be helpful. Providing support and advice gets people so much further than providing reasons why people didn't do what you wanted or expected. It's about moving forward and getting things done. In every situation you have a choice. Am I going to be a victim or am I going to be an owner? I choose owner and it takes effort, but the effort is rewarded.

Simple Success Strategy: Become an Owner

Some people may be prone to going into either the victim or ownership mentality, but that doesn't mean they are bad people. It does mean that people who go into a victim mentality are more likely to be labeled as complainers and less productive, and that has a negative impact on the people around them. At the same time, if someone is more likely to go toward an ownership mindset, they are thought of as a star employee and tend to have stronger upward mobility during their careers. The following is a roadmap that outlines two pathways that you have the power to choose from. One is an identity of a victim who things happen to and the other is an owner who makes things happen. Both of them start at the same place, with an event, and they end up in very different places with different outcomes.

The Event

The event is the situation, change, or activity. This does not have to be something as major as an organizational change or life change. It can be something minor, such as a new employee entering your team or a decision that is made that you don't agree with. You do not have direct control over the event, but you do have direct control on how you respond.

The Decision

The decision is the most important part of the pathway to ownership—period! The decision is about choice. It's what you have direct control over. The reason it's the most important part of the pathway is that it sets your direction and, quite often, others will follow. It's the pivot point, the point at which you spark movement. Just like the law of inertia, once you start in a certain direction, you tend to stay moving in that direction. However, you can make a new decision at any point during the pathway and shift direction toward ownership.

The Victim Cycle

The victim cycle is a process in which a person gets caught up in moving away from ownership. We all fall into a victim cycle from time to time. The key to become effective at identifying warning signs and understanding the impact it has on you and others. When people enter into the victim cycle, they are focused on what others aren't doing rather than on what they can be doing in order to adapt or to get ahead. To put it simply, they get stuck by themselves about themselves.

Reject. The first phase in the victim cycle is rejecting. This is when you are not on board with the event and you are resisting it. Think of this as saying "No" even before you know. In this phase, you are bracing yourself to push back, or worse, be a silent derailer. Rejecting does not have to be something that is dramatic and observable. Someone may be rejecting the event and not talking about it at all. The reject phase is when you are not aligned with the event or simply don't want anything to change because you are quite comfortable.

Redirect and blame. This phase is about trying to take the heat off yourself and getting it on others, even if there is no one else involved. Often, people have trained themselves to blame others, the organization, or the system. When stress is high, redirection and blame become even higher. This means that people who are stuck in the victim cycle gain comfort from talking about what isn't going right, rather than what can go right.

Rationalize. The rationalize phase is about trying to make it true for you. People will naturally try to make sense of situations and support their victim mentality. One of the most dangerous parts of the rationalize phase is that it often becomes a way to recruit other victims or to put more weight on people with an ownership mentality. Human nature is to support others when they are in need. If someone is resisting an event and/or blaming others and talking about it, other victims will join the pity party. The danger here is that a victim alliance can be created and, even if it's not intentional, can be actively counterproductive to the success of an organizational initiative. In the case of an event that isn't organizational and is just personal, a victim alliance can help reinforce why you can't adapt rather than what you can do to adapt.

Retract. The retract phase is about disengagement. People get good at RIP, "retiring in place." It's not always as dramatic as shutting down completely; it can be as simple as someone not taking action to move forward or getting complacent. When I was at Springfield College's Athletic Counseling Program, renowned sport psychiatrist Dr. Burt Giges taught me that when you retract and avoid, you leave a void. This stuck with me and has proven to be true. If you retract taking ownership, you will not learn or grow, nor will you advance in your professional or personal life.

The good news about being in the victim cycle is you can always decide to go in a different direction. Some people get very good at catching themselves becoming a victim and making a shift.

The Ownership Cycle

Accept. The accept phase sets the tone and direction toward an ownership mentality. If you accept what has happened, you step toward what will happen. If someone accepts the event or change, it doesn't necessarily mean they agree with it, it just means they are ready to deal with it. Their energy moves toward action rather than reaction.

Attitude. Once you recall that you are in control of you, your attitude shifts. You gain more focus. It is important to stay positive despite setbacks. Your positive attitude will provide fuel for what is to come. You will start to reap the rewards of a positive attitude as you move forward. Though it may not always be the easiest thing to do, it is the most effective and the most rewarding.

The Pathway To Ownership

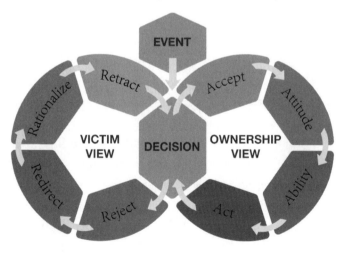

EVENT

Retract   Accept

Rationalize   Attitude

VICTIM VIEW   DECISION   OWNERSHIP VIEW

Redirect   Ability

Reject   Act

2015 © Rob Fazio, PhD
OnPoint Advising, Inc

Ability. Ability is about developing the skills you need to move forward. You may already have the skills to tackle what challenges the new event presents or you may need to further develop them. In this phase, you want to ask yourself what do you know and what do you need to know. New challenges often call for new skills. People who are in the ability phase focus on learning what they need to move forward, or ask for help from someone who already knows.

Act. Nothing breeds confidence like small wins. Taking action toward something is much more powerful than hiding or moving away from something. People with an ownership mentality act intentionally and focus forward rather than backward.

The key to success around moving forward is getting skilled at knowing when you fall into the victim trap and how to get yourself into an ownership mindset. The more ownership you take, the more progress you will make. The next level of ownership is being able to identify when others around you fall into a victim mindset and helping them get into an ownership mindset.

5

Thinking Errors
Mind Muscle Memory

W e all make mistakes. It's part of life. However, we don't all learn from our mistakes and we all don't learn when we are making mistakes so we can prevent future mishaps. Through the course of the day, we are very comfortable with making typos and errors. It's pretty simple: you make a typo, you notice it, and you correct it.

We don't have the same discipline when it comes to our thinking patterns. It's not a normal and natural process to pay attention to how we think and if we are being irrational. Sometimes, irrational thinking becomes so frequent that it creates anxiety or eats away at our confidence. During the course of the day, we all have irrational thoughts pop in and out of our minds. Irrational thoughts are common and become thinking errors. Thinking errors are thoughts that we feel are real, but they are just thoughts that we give power to. They happen so fast that they become an automatic response. If we are not careful, they become our reality.

The renowned psychologist Albert Ellis gave a tremendous gift to mankind when he taught people about cognitive behavioral therapy. The basic premise for this process is that your thinking impacts your feelings and your behaviors. Therefore, if you can learn how to prevent thinking errors, you can guide your feelings and behaviors to be more focused on the positive.

Taking this a step further, if you put the time into creating positive thought patterns, you can literally train yourself to be more positive and focused. This comes into play on a daily basis. Let's take an example of someone who needs to perform well when giving a presentation. Prior to that presentation, a person may get so consumed with worrying about what may go wrong that they don't focus on the core message they want to deliver or prepare themselves for success by building their confidence.

In my work with athletes advising them on mental toughness and sport psychology techniques, I learned about the power of muscle memory. Baseball players spend hours upon hours fine tuning their craft of batting. It's a combination of art and science. They take batting practice, study situations, study pitchers, study pitches, and develop an ingrained muscle memory that allows them to put thinking on the shelf so they can perform in the moment. Put simply, they not only rule out thinking errors, but are also so prepared, practiced, and respond so quickly that they don't have to rely on their thinking at all. The best of the best recognize a release and their bodies take over. It doesn't mean that they are always going to execute to perfection, but it means they lower the margin of error because they are prepared. They know what to expect, what to look for, and how to swing accordingly. This muscle memory has great power. In a sense, they are able to temporarily remove mental barriers so they can swing without thought and let their muscle memory take over and perform as they have trained. In fact, when slumps occur, it's often because something doesn't feel right, and when things don't feel right, they begin to have thinking errors leading to a domino effect.

Simple Success Strategy: Mind Muscle Memory

Although raw talent in sport and business goes a long way, it's not the raw talent that is the differentiator. It's the preparation, repetition, and focus that win the day. One of the greatest public examples of the power of not giving in to thinking errors and relying on preparation and focus comes from the 2015 Super Bowl. The New England Patriots were playing the Seattle Seahawks and it looked like the Seahawks were about to win it all. They were in scoring position. All they needed to do was to hand the ball off to their all-pro running back to score as they had done all season.

Twenty seconds before the 2015 Super Bowl ended, no one knew who Patriots defensive player Malcolm Butler was. Now, we all want to know how he did it. Butler's interception came as we were all convinced the game was over. He'll be remembered as the man who changed the fate of the game. It wasn't his hands that made the play—it was his head. His head is what gave him the opportunity to make a moment count. The undrafted rookie corner from a Division 2 school set himself up for success. He put together a demonstration of four key mental skills: rehearse, refocus, recognize, and react.

Rehearse

The best athletes have a common, critical characteristic: *mental muscle memory.* Our minds are like an app. If you program it, it will respond accordingly. If you don't, anything can happen. Baseball players spend countless hours in batting practice so they can, in mere seconds, react to a pitch. In martial arts, athletes program themselves with a foundation of blocking and striking. They don't have to think, because their muscle memory takes over. In practice, Butler rehearsed the very play in which he made the interception.

Refocus

Mental muscle memory includes the ability to override any noise and refocus. A few plays prior to the interception, Butler was the player who was covering Seattle's wide receiver, Jermaine Kearse, who made a spectacular and highlight-reel catch. At that moment Butler was the guy who got beat. When Seattle lined up for the goal line play, Butler wasn't even going to be on the field because New England was in their defense base. However, when Seattle put in an extra receiver, Butler got put in the game. Butler was resilient enough to embrace the pressure and rely on his instincts and assignment. Plenty of athletes would have still been focused on the last missed opportunity. However, Butler was refocused. In sport psychology, it's called having temporary amnesia. You need to be able to forget what has been done and focus on what to do.

Recognize

All of us fans of the game were certain it would be Seattle's running back Marshawn Lynch to run the ball at a half yard out, but Butler stayed disciplined. Because he rehearsed and prepared, he knew what it would look like if Seattle was going to try to set up a pass play. He didn't get caught up in the distractions. He recognized what was about to happen before it happened.

React

A reaction is something that is automatic. You don't think, you perform. Butler's nickname, "Scrap," also played a role. He was someone who was always around the ball and ready to intervene to make a play. He was someone who had a mindset that took smart risks. In that key moment, Butler didn't question himself, he went with his gut, reacted, and jumped the route. This means he recognized the route the wide receiver was running and got to the ball before the receiver did.

Though most executives will never even attend a Super Bowl, this can serve as a powerful lesson to teach us about which mental muscle memories we build every day. If you are someone who is a student of the game of business, you can learn to prepare so when opportunities arise, you capitalize.

Here's the danger. If you aren't aware of how you are programmed, you can build mental muscle memory that will actually hold you back or, worse, have you reacting in a negative way. When you don't have time to pause and think about your next step, you better be programmed to recognize and react in the right direction. Why is the right direction so critical? In a word: brand. Before Butler's "moment," he had a brand, one that was not intentional. The brand was one of a guy who shouldn't be on the field with the game on the line—an undrafted rookie, a walk-on that just let up the pass to Kearse that ended the Patriots' season.

When a brand or story is created, people see things through that lens and look to reinforce it. Once this happens, changing that brand is tough, very tough. You need a combination of key factors to rewrite the story leading to a different brand. This can be done in two ways. The first involves a lot of time, intentional behavior change, and impression management. The second is simple: a game-changing event.

If you need more evidence of how to perform under pressure, see Sully Sullenberger of the "Miracle on the Hudson," who reacted well and saved lives. Although there are several well-known examples of rising to the occasion and being at the pinnacle of success under pressure, we all have the power to do this. The more we are aware of our thinking errors, the more we can replace them with a pathway to success and optimal performance. What's the point? Build your mind's muscle today, so when pivotal moments arise, you let your head lead your hands. Will you hesitate and let someone else get in the end zone? Or, will you jump the route?

6

Getting Stuck in Reverse
Shifting Gears

W here we focus is where we go. This chapter is about
getting results through focusing forward and not
getting stuck. Five years ago, two of my close friends who
were into skiing asked me to start coming on some trips
with them. Because I wasn't a big skier, I had the brilliant
idea of picking up snowboarding. My thinking was based
on what I heard, the learning curve was steep, but once
you got it, you got it, and your skill accelerates fast. Well, I
had a different experience.

I had the toughest time getting to a place where
I could go down the mountain or bunny slope without
great fear. Despite several lessons and some practice, a tip

I got in a random conversation was most helpful. The person told me, where you focus is where you go. It seemed ridiculous and simple at the time, but when I started to put it into practice, it worked. I was spending so much time preparing for my falls or worrying about where not to go (that is, trees), that I wasn't focusing on where to go. Once I started to look where I wanted to go, I spent less time ending up in places I didn't want to be. Now that we know it's important to focus on where we want to go, let's walk through how to do it.

Simple Success Strategy: Shifting Gears Through Self-Advising and Self-Questioning

Our mindset is what sets our direction. I like to use the metaphor of driving a car. You have control over what gear you are in and the direction you are going. You can choose to put the car in drive, neutral, or reverse. As you would gather, it's very difficult to get to a desired destination in reverse. Self-advising is designed to help you focus forward and stay in drive. I am not saying that you can never be in reverse. However, the longer you are in reverse, the longer you focus on moving away from success rather than toward success. Knowing how to get yourself from reverse (negative thinking) to neutral and neutral to drive (positive thinking) will serve you well.

We won't have to look too far to see examples of how shifting gears and focus can make an impact. The best athletes deal with adversity and losing by learning how to bounce back. Athletes use a range of skills to develop their mental toughness. Self-advising is one strategy that is the difference between the athletes who "want to take the final shot" and those who "drop the ball."

Athletes who are at their best when things are at their worst have little to do with their physical talent or intellectual horsepower. It's about resilience, grit, and toughness. The best athletes pay attention to their inner coach and advise themselves how to focus. We all seek guidance and coaching from others. At the same time, you are the only person you will be with every moment of your life. Therefore, it makes sense to become good at advising yourself. The key to self-advising is being aware of what you say to yourself in key moments that can put you in reverse. A classic example of this is the difference between how Michael Jordan used to play the game and how others played. When Jordan missed a shot, you rarely saw him put his head down and demonstrate that he was focusing on the miss. He shifted gears fast and focused on playing defense and getting ready for the next shot. He didn't let himself get stuck in reverse; he focused on the next shot.

Change Your Assumptions to Responses

Following is a simple strategy to help you stay focused on moving forward and toward your goals. Let's take the example of budget cuts to illustrate the benefit of coaching yourself. The framework EAR will help you be intentional about what you hear. I realize that the acronym EAR can seem hokey, but if there is one thing I have learned is that what people remember is what people use. It is a strategy to help you reframe what happens to you so you can focus forward.

E—Event: The event or situation.

A—Assumption: Your initial thoughts, beliefs, or feelings in relation to the event.

R—Result: The consequence; what happens.

The trap that people fall into is that they believe the result is a direct outcome of the event. In reality, it is our assumption about the event that creates the outcome. Take a look at the following example.

Event:

→   Lack of hitting monthly sales numbers.

Assumption:

→   "We are never going to get out of this mess."
→   "No one on the sales team is focused on results."
→   "I am not a good leader."

Result:

→   Feelings of self-doubt.
→   Focus on fear of what is going to happen next.
→   Snowball effect of negative thinking.
→   Lower confidence and motivation.
→   Focus on what you can't control.

It is natural to automatically assume that the event (in this case, not hitting the sales numbers) causes the consequence. However, in reality, your assumption or belief about the event is what causes the result. With self-advising, the emphasis is on shifting your assumption to something that will work for you rather than against you. Here is an example of shifting a negative assumption to a positive one.

Event:

→ Lack of hitting monthly sales numbers.

Assumption (shifting to helpful thinking):

→ "This is a tough situation and it's an opportunity to see how I can help myself focus on a solution."
→ "What can I learn from what led to this month's numbers?"
→ "Not hitting the numbers is going to present some challenges. I'll be able to see who handles pressure well and who creates more challenges."
→ "I am disappointed in the numbers. What do I need to do to prevent this from happening next month?"
→ "I put in a lot of effort and came up short. Who do I need to have direct conversations with in the next couple of days?"

Result:

→ Emphasis is on acceptance and action.
→ Create momentum of positive thinking.
→ Maintaining confidence and motivation.
→ Focus is on what you can control.

This skill of self-advising includes areas of reframing and will help you focus forward and decrease your chances of going in reverse. It will also train you to create a more positive attitude with time. It will help you move more quickly toward action. Your thoughts, feelings, and actions all work together. Reframing sets you up to focus forward, especially when something happens that can put you in reverse.

Self-Questioning: The Answer Is in What You Ask

Earlier we focused on self-advising and what you tell yourself. Now we are going to focus on what you ask yourself. This strategy is a foundation for what I teach athletes and executives. At first, people seem to resist the idea that you can train your brain through the questions you ask yourself, but once they get it, it makes an impact.

Our minds are complex smartphones. The good news is you don't need to be a software engineer to program positive habits in yourself. A smartphone works best when it has good input and so does your mind. Pay attention to the questions you ask yourself. Redirect yourself and ensure that you ask yourself positive and strength-based questions. For example, rather than asking, "Why am I never getting asked to take on key responsibilities at work?" try asking yourself, "What are the people who are getting asked to take on key responsibilities doing?" The shift may be subtle, but it gets you focusing forward and on what you can influence. The following are some additional positive questions you can ask yourself:

→ What do I need to do to build my credibility?
→ What skills do I want to develop this year?

→ What did I learn from that tough experience?

→ Who can I help now so they won't make the same mistake I did?

→ How can I help other people?

→ Who can I get support from to help me accelerate my career?

→ What do I want to focus on that will be beneficial to the business and myself?

Whether you know it or not, we all talk to ourselves and it has an impact. Inner dialogue is one conversation where we have control over what is said and how it is received. Self-advising and self-questioning are ways to take an active role in your pathway to success and on staying focused. You will find that, with time, you will develop positive habits that help you find the positive in situations. You have the power to direct your line of thinking, just like I learned the power of redirecting myself to focus on where I wanted to go when I snowboard (the course), rather than if anyone would find me when I crashed into a tree. Spending a little time every day paying attention to what you ask and what you tell yourself will go a long way.

Section 2

Reading

7

Listening Is Bad for Your Health

Selective Listening and Talking Back

As an adviser to executives, I am constantly reminding influential people with power that listening and understanding is critical to leadership success. I know this chapter name is a huge risk. The truth is that listening is important, but it can also hold you back and be the cause of many bad decisions. We all hear messages as we go up the ladder, and many of them have served us well. For example, hearing from a boss, "You have the talent to be a successful executive" is a message we can benefit from. At the same time, we have all heard messages that have served as limitations.

Why does a two-ton circus elephant not just pull the little stake out of the ground and run free? The answer is so simple, yet creates complexity. As young elephants, they are secured to a rope attached to a stake in the ground. The elephants try at a young age to move forward and pull the stake out of the ground, but are unsuccessful. With time, the elephants learn that they are not able to break free, and they stop trying.

This example applies to all of us! We tend to crystalize negative messages and learn to stop trying. A personal example of this is when I was young. I had a hard time with the math problems marked by the little star that indicated they were the most difficult. I was encouraged to skip them because they would take me too much time and I would likely not figure them out. So what did I do every time I saw a hard question? I gave up. I learned to not even try. It wasn't until later on in life that I realized I was holding myself back. Every time I hear myself say, "You won't be able to do this," I reframe it and take on the challenge with an open mind.

These messages, which I refer to as *barrier beliefs*, inhibit our potential. I was recently talking with an executive who believed he wasn't good at strategy. When we talked further, it turned out that he was actually very strategic, but just became intimidated any time he needed to *be* strategic. Instead of realizing this distinction, he accepted this limitation and did little to combat it. The perfect storm of barrier creation is hearing a message early on and not having strong enough self-esteem or mentoring to pull you away from the belief. I've seen it ruin careers and, worse, ruin lives. These barrier beliefs become mental models. We don't know as much about the brain as we know about the body, but we know that the mind can put limitations on us that stick. It's natural and normal for them to become our primary source of limitations.

Another example of when someone pushed back on her barrier beliefs is Amy Cuddy, a business professor at Harvard. She conducts research on how our nonverbal behaviors can override our negative responses to stress and, instead, make us perceive and behave in more powerful ways. Although her work speaks to the topic at hand, what really resonates with barrier beliefs started with a car accident during her sophomore year in college. Cuddy sustained such significant injuries that her IQ dropped two standard deviations. This diagnosis was particularly heartbreaking to Cuddy because she identified with being an intelligent person. In fact, she had been called a "gifted" child because of her high IQ. After her accident, her medical team encouraged her to quit school. She was advised to find other passions and ways to make a living. However Cuddy, who refused to lose the part of her identity she most valued, decided not to listen. Instead, she worked hard. She took twice as long to finish college, but she also found herself at Princeton for graduate work, hired by Harvard, and with one of the most watched TED Talks in recent history. If Cuddy had listened to her medical team, she never would have overcome her injuries and enjoyed these accomplishments. Instead, the message that she wasn't smart enough to finish school would have become a barrier belief. These negative messages are rampant in the business world and they can easily transform into barrier beliefs.

Another example is of a person who was told that he "lacked imagination and had no good ideas." He was fired from the well-known newspaper, *The Kansas City Star.* Wow, could you imagine being fired for lack of imagination from a newspaper? You would think imagination is low on the list in that job description. Another person was a woman who got fired from the evening news for being too emotionally connected to the stories. Instead of embracing her compassion, she was being reprimanded for not delivering news in a disconnected way. These are just two examples of when messages have the potential to override people's perceptions of themselves. In just a bit, I'll share how well these two people dealt with the tough messages they were sent, but first let's focus on what to do so barriers don't control you.

Simple Success Strategy: Selective Listening and Talking Back

There are indirect and direct approaches to manage what limitations you are putting on yourself. An indirect approach would be to just wait and see what happens. This is what most people do: go through life and progress throughout their careers until a limitation becomes a liability. These challenges often arise when it's too late and you miss opportunities or get passed by for a job promotion. Another indirect manifestation of barrier beliefs is projecting them onto others. In these cases, your insecurities affect, and often limit, the people around you.

Let's take another example of an executive I was advising. This person learned throughout his life that it's not smart to trust people because when you aren't paying attention, they will betray you. This resulted in this executive constantly micromanaging his staff and creating an environment where there was a lack of trust. When he became the boss of a group of highly effective employees, he literally decreased their productivity. After months of the team feeling like they weren't trusted, they stopped having confidence in their boss and eventually in one another. The common barrier belief then became, "You can't trust people." Rather than the team collaborating, their lack of trust diminished productivity and resulted in negative outcomes for the business. This example is an extreme case. However, all of us have impact—whether we realize it or not. That's why it's critical to take a direct approach to identifying and replacing the beliefs that bind us. We all have these beliefs, but we don't all have to fall victim to their manipulation.

The direct approach is about *awareness* and *action*. The first step is to identify what messages you have heard throughout your childhood or career that have created barrier beliefs. Remember that these messages are not facts, they are just messages. We have the choice to listen or not. Ask yourself, "Where did I learn this?" and "What can I do to break free from this limitation?" The more you focus on what you can do rather than on what you can't do, the more successful you will be. You will also find yourself having less stress and more energy.

Once you are aware of your barrier beliefs, take action to override them. This can be done by leveraging the Awareness and Action table on page 91 to map out what you are doing, or not doing, as a result of your beliefs. Going back to my math example from my childhood, I didn't feel smart enough to attempt to answer the hard questions. I was shutting down and not trying when things were challenging. I became self-defeating and exemplified the opposite of perseverance. I was passive and let my automatic beliefs create my future rather than creating it for myself.

So how is listening bad for your health? Language is very strong and our inner dialogue is either our fuel to move forward or an anchor that keeps us stuck. Worse, it can create a cycle of self-defeat and worry that has an impact on our emotional and physical well-being. Paying attention to what we say to ourselves as a result of what others have said to us can be the difference between the elephant that stays stuck and the one that pulls the stake out of the ground and roams free. The following is a snapshot of how you can leverage your awareness to take positive action.

Shifting Your Belief Barriers to Motivators

It's time to tell you who the two mystery people are from the earlier examples. If you remember, person one was a man who was fired because he was told he lacked imagination and person two was a woman who was fired because she was too emotionally connected to the people in the news stories she reported. Who are the two? Have you heard of Walt Disney and Oprah? Now they are examples of what can happen when you have selective listening and talk back! Walt Disney's story is a great example of someone being fired for what he had and people didn't see. Now that's dangerous. Could you imagine if Walt Disney

Awareness/Action Table

Awareness		Action	
Message	• You aren't smart and you don't "get it."	New Message	• Your skills are unique and you excel in different areas.
Belief	• I don't fit in and I'm always going to be steps behind other people.	New Belief	• I can leverage what I value, what I'm good at, and what makes me feel confident.
Limitations	• Fear of learning. • Giving up before I start.	New Opportunity	• Find the synergy between what I love to do, what I am skilled at, and what people need.
Result	• Defeated. • Lack of motivation and confidence.	New Result	• Focus on what I can control. • Comfortable with taking risks. • Confident. • Passionate about helping others help themselves.

listened and didn't break through what he was told? As for Oprah, her story is an example of a boss who didn't recognize what talent looked like. This happens more often than not. People see things through their experiences and can have a narrow view of success. Who do you want to be known as: the person who fired Walt and Oprah or the person who broke through their belief barriers?

8

The Blind Side
Mind Your Blind Side

What if you didn't know what was holding you back? What if despite your best efforts and hours of time, your career didn't progress or, worse, consistently went backward? One of the most difficult parts of my work is helping people "to get" what they "don't get." Let me share with you the story of Linda.

Linda was a hard worker and she had a lot of success for years in a Fortune 500 organization. She was known as someone who could identify what was wrong and fix it. She was valued for her straightforward approach and ability to enhance the potential of the group. Linda got hired away to another organization.

This was a tremendous opportunity for Linda because she loves what she does and was going to make a lot of money doing what she does best—finding problems and fixing them. She was one of the best at constant improvement. As a Black Belt in Six Sigma, which is an approach to eliminating waste and defects in a process, Linda was also thrilled because she was getting a big pay raise in her new job and would be managing several people.

Sounds like a great story of success brewing, right? Wrong. Within six months of her new job, Linda was taken off every major project, her direct reports were taken away from her, and she was never told why. I met Linda after her career had already derailed and was asked to provide her feedback and coach her.

Linda had no clue how she came across to people. Frankly, Linda rubbed just about everyone the wrong way. She didn't understand that she didn't need to improve every single thing. From her point of view, she was just doing what she thought she was hired to do. From the point of view of others, she was annoying and had no idea what others thought of her.

Unfortunately, Linda had what we call a blind spot, and a huge one. We all have blind spots, which are things that others can see but we don't. The danger of having blind spots is that you can become the master of unintended consequences. In Linda's case, she thought she was constantly adding value, but in reality, she was constantly diminishing value.

I've seen this happen many times. The unfortunate part is that Linda was really right and had business appropriate solutions to offer. The problem was that she was such a turn off that people stopped listening to her. In the simplest form, Linda was getting in the way of her brilliance. Not only did people not want to listen to her, people didn't want to be around her.

So what is a blind spot? A blind spot is something you say, do, or demonstrate that has an impact that you are not aware of, but others are. The best way to describe this in a typical setting is if you have a piece of broccoli in your teeth at a cocktail party and everyone can see it, except you. It doesn't mean it's not there and it's not making an impact. It just means you're the one not seeing it.

Johari Window

The Johari window is an incredibly useful tool and simple visual that teaches people the importance of being self-aware. Two psychologists, Joseph Luft and Harry Ingham, created it in 1955 studying groups at UCLA. It's a great example of how simplicity can lead to effectiveness. Successful people intentionally decrease the size of their blind spots. It's a process that takes time, not an event.

	Characteristics Known to Others	Characteristics Unknown to Others
Characteristics Known to Leader	Public areas	Private areas
Characteristics Unknown to Leader	Leadership blind spots	Subconscious

Simple Success Strategy: Mind your Blind Side

The hit movie, *The Blind Side*, was about a real-life, talented football player that worked hard and found his way to the National Football League. The name of the movie is what is relevant for this simple strategy. In football, one of the most important people on the field is the offensive lineman who protects the quarterback's blind side. In other words, he protects the quarterback from where he can't see. If a quarterback throws with his right hand, he naturally faces to the right of the field and therefore can't see defenders blitzing from the left side because his back is to them. What can be learned from this metaphor? First, find your blind side and second, have someone you trust protect your blind side so you don't get unexpectedly knocked down, or worse, injured.

Find Your Blind Side

Awareness is the first step toward action that leads us toward success. This section of the book is all about *Reading*, which is about learning and understanding. Keep your focus on uncovering and understanding what you do or what can happen that can lead to your demise. Using the earlier example of Linda, her blind side is that she believes she is always adding value when just the opposite is true; she is actually diminishing value because her delivery masks the message. Here are a few questions you can use to find your blind side:

→   What do other people say about you in jest?
→   What don't I get asked to do that I want
     to do?

These questions are good indicators of some blind spots that may have emerged. As we know, often things said in jest are an indirect way to give people feedback.

Protect Your Blind Side

Once you know what your blind side looks like, you can take action to protect it. The most direct way is to have people who are candid tell you how it is, early and often. However, asking for feedback seldom happens. There are two guidelines that will help you get direct and accurate feedback. The first one is in the way you ask and the second is in the way you deliver feedback.

When you ask for feedback, think of it as creating a new norm of transparent communication. Don't ask, "Do you have any feedback?" or "How do you think that went?" A better way to present this is by saying something such as, "I am working on getting better at being more direct and concise in my communication. What are 1–2 tips that you can give me on how I can improve my communication?" This approach gives you a higher probability of actually getting some valid information. Keep in mind, the more senior you are in an organization, the less you get it and the more you need it.

The second guideline to help you get more direct feedback is to give direct feedback. You can be clear and kind. If you consistently guide people, give them advice, and give them feedback, they will be more likely to give you feedback and, best of all, protect your blind side.

Repeat

The interesting thing about having a blind spot is that we become very good at forgetting about them, ignoring them, or creating new ones. Think about it. Every time you take on a new job, new adventure, or new challenge, you run the risk of new blind spots popping up. The best thing you can do is to make this a continuous process and have people around you who will point out your blind spots.

The action you take at decreasing your blind spot and decreasing the blind spots of others will have a direct impact on your success. It is much harder to get derailed through the course of your career if you know where the barriers are on the tracks.

9

Bad Advice

Create a Constellation of Competence

We are all under pressure—pressure to perform, pressure to conform to a culture, and pressure to listen to others. There is no doubt that advice is critical to success. However, it's not just advice that is critical; it's advice from the right people at the right time. Let's be honest, advice people give is based on other people's preferences and their priorities. If you don't keep that on top of your mind, things can go terribly wrong. What has been evident to me through the years is that people get some really bad advice at some really bad times. Why is this? It's because people in need tend to go with solutions based on who they like rather than who has expertise.

One of the interviews for this book included a conversation with Reuben Daniels, who is the Cofounder of EA Markets and former Co-head of U.S. Investment Banking with Barclays Capital. When I asked Reuben what was the most simple, yet helpful success strategy he could offer people he said, "Have a mentor." Though many of us have heard of the importance of having a mentor, when someone who has been as successful as Reuben says it, it carries more weight.

Reuben explained that a common characteristic that he has seen in others who are successful is that they have had sponsorship through the years. He used the metaphor of walking in deep snow. Although you may be able to do it on your own, one can cover much more ground walking in the steps of someone who has set the path. It's about finding someone who can create clarity for your path and guide you in the right direction. Something that was fascinating to learn from Reuben was he said that intellectual horsepower alone wasn't enough for success. He explained to me that banking is a team sport and every player benefits from a coach that looks out for you and who has influence; a person who can not only guide you through the snow, but can also protect you from the crevasses when needed.

I know what most people would be interested in next. We know having a mentor is important, but how do we get one? In my view, it is not a formal process and it is not about getting "one." It's about creating a constellation of competence.

Simple Success Strategy: Create a Constellation of Competence

How do you create a constellation of competence? Through an intentional and direct approach with clear decision rules. Too often people take advice from the first person that will provide it or just because they are friends. Although excellent advice can come from the person sitting next to you on a train or your best friend, it's often the case that the person giving you advice has no idea what they are talking about. Different points of view from different types of people can be very beneficial. That's why it's important to have a number of people you can go to. There are three core questions you should ask yourself about the people you get advice from: Are they credible? Are they candid? Are they connected?

Are They Credible?

Credibility is earned and comes through a track record of consistently positive behavior. Someone with credibility has a strong reputation. They have a reputation for doing what is right and when it's right, not just a reputation for "winning" or making money. When you ask yourself, "Is this person credible?" the answer should come pretty quickly. Someone who is credible is someone who others are eager to follow.

Are They Candid?

There is nothing more important in your personal and business life than having people around you who will tell you the truth. The more successful you become, the more feedback you will need, and the less you will get it. I get paid to give truth to people in power because those working with them are fearful of the repercussions and often limit the feedback they offer those higher up. The truth is, sometimes it is smart to hold your tongue and hold off on giving advice. However, you want to have people around you who are not afraid. A close friend and former colleague of mine, Todd Alexander, wrote an article called, "Getting Stabbed in the Front." I think the message from the article is brilliant. We all need people around us who are willing to tell us like it is and give their honest and candid point of view.

Are They Connected?

If someone is connected, they care about you and your success. These people are on your team, know where you want to go, and want to help you get there. If someone is connected, they are aligned with your passion and you know it. Within my personal constellation of competence, Joy Zaben, the Chief of Staff for Capital One Retail Bank, is someone who I recognize as connected. She is one of the strongest advocates for people's passion inside and outside of her professional responsibilities. She is the type of person who can shift a culture to focus on collective wins. No matter what transition I am presented with, I know I can trust that she is on my team and will look out for what is best for my future. Keep in mind that just because someone is connected, it does not mean that they always agree with you. It just means that they are on your team and their intention is to help you have your desired impact.

Because Joy has been a success in every role she has taken on, I asked her what helpful, yet simple success strategy she had for people. On a side note, I have spoken with dozens of people who have told me that Joy has changed their lives for the better and gives the best advice. Joy talked about the importance of helping people by making sure you see things from their perspective first. It was certainly good advice and advice I had heard before. I thought to myself, okay, so she is saying to be empathetic and understand the other person's perspective. What she said next had a profound impact on me and opened my eyes up to something I need to do better when I coach executives. Joy summed up her simple success strategy with very pointed advice. She said, *"If you truly want to walk in someone else's shoes, you have to take your shoes off first!"* It was a great lesson on ensuring that when you give advice, make sure you are giving advice that is based on what the person needs, not what you do.

The three core characteristics, credibility, candidness, and connectedness, are standards for people you elect to your constellation. People who have a combination of these characteristics not only give great advice, they also help build your brand by association. If you have alliances with people who possess these attributes, chances are they will help you get to places you want to go. The next step is to be part of other people's constellation of competence. Are you credible? Are you candid? Are you connected? If you are, then it's likely you will get the same in return.

10

Thinking Too Much or Too Little About What People Think
Intentional Impressions

W hat do you mean I need to have a brand; isn't that for businesses?" This is the question I hear when I advise people on developing a brand. What I tell them is that whether they know it or not, they have a brand. We all do. People have perceptions of you and they stick. If people don't know the story, they will make one up and it's often a lot worse than the actual story. This holds true for organizations and people.

Just like much in life, it's a balancing act. The people who focus too much on what others think get branded as political animals, overly ambitious, or "worry warts." People who don't think about what others think at all are the ones who are left wondering why the people around them are getting opportunities and they aren't. In my experience, people don't give enough thought or time to what other people think of them. It amazes me, because if we look at the world it's easy to see that brands drive behavior. Brands are the motivating factor for whether we purchase something or pick a different item or service.

What's the difference between FedEx and the U.S. Postal Service? One of them you expect to deliver; the other you expect an excuse. They both provide the same service, but one has built a brand on a statement, "When it absolutely, positively has to be there overnight." That statement is powerful. It's powerful because anyone in business understands the importance of something getting somewhere when it absolutely has to get there. What's more important is that FedEx backs up their brand with getting it done. They live up to their statement. In brands we trust.

Let me give you two examples of people brands I often come across: "The Nice Person" and "The Open Door Guy." The nice person is the one that everyone thinks of as being nice before they think of him or her as anything else. I've worked with several people who were so cordial they were never clear. The unfortunate thing is that often people who have the "Nice Person" brand are brilliant, but people don't leverage them because they don't hear their point of view. These people are also easily bulldozed.

The open door guy is the person who is usually clueless. He often comes to me and says something such as, "I don't know why people say I'm not approachable. I have an open door policy." Newsflash: an open door means nothing if you are intimidating and are overly forceful. This is the guy who people talk about rather than talk with. He often gets his way, not because of people's respect, but because people fear him or don't want to deal with him.

If you don't let people know who you are, they will be happy to tell you. Businesses spend countless dollars providing their employees with feedback. The concept is a good one. The focus is on helping people learn how they come across to others.

Simple Success Strategy: Intentional Impressions

A brand comes from the consistency of your behavior and confidence other people have in you to continue to be consistent. The best example I can think of is Dr. John Gates, cofounder of Avion Consulting. He works with top caliber talent around the world. His brand is bullet proof. No matter who you talk to, no matter what the circumstance, you know you will get transparency. The man oozes credibility. I'm confident his brand is a key factor in why banks around the world seek to work with him.

Creating a brand is a balancing act between being intentional and being genuine. The reason it is a balancing act is that if you try too hard and are too overt about creating your brand, a brand of being self-serving or being overly ambitious can be attributed to you. The way to create a brand is to create intentional impressions in a genuine way. There are four core aspects of intentional impressions: aspiration, awareness, activity, and attention.

Aspiration

This is all about intention. Know what you want people to think, say, and feel about you. Start with something simple that you can deliver on. An example may be being reliable, focused, candid, and courageous. Identify three to five descriptors that capture what your aspirational brand is. Once you have your descriptors, take it a step further and identify a couple of phrases that you want people to say about you. An example of this is, "Reese has so much depth on digital transformation and she is someone we can count on to tell it like it is." It's all about the "sound bite." Make it easy for people to talk to you and to be able to talk about you. If you can clearly communicate your intentional brand, then so can others. If you aren't able to articulate it, then others won't be able to either.

Awareness

If you don't know what people say about you, then there is a good chance they are saying things you don't want them to say. Take some time to think about what others think. It doesn't mean you need to be consumed with what others think, but you do want it to be on your radar. By "be on your radar," I mean you are aware and can determine whether or not it is of value or just noise that holds you back. Ask some people in your professional and personal life to tell you how they would describe you to others. It's important to include people you tend to click with as well as people who you haven't clicked with. The idea is to get a sense of where the gap is between your aspirational brand and your current brand. Keep in mind that people are hesitant to give direct feedback. The more you can find people who aren't afraid to tell you like it is, the better. Another strategy is to ask someone else who you trust to collect some of this information for you.

Activity

Activity is all about action. The equation is simple: when you act a certain way, people see you in a certain way. The worst thing people can do for their brand is talk about what people should do and then do something else. No one wants to be associated with that person. Identify what you need to do to create the impressions you want others to see in you. If you don't know, think about people who have a brand you admire and figure out what they do that makes you think that way. There is no substitute for activity.

Attention

Once you know what you want (aspiration), what you are getting (awareness), and what you need to do (activity), you can focus. Focus on who and what can help you turn around or enhance your brand. I have found that the people you align with contribute to your brand. Although you can't control what people say about you, you can control who you spend your time with and who you support. The best thing you can do for your brand is build relationships with people who have influence. An effective strategy can be to let people know what your aspirational brand is and to ask them for their help.

The most direct path to a brand is an indirect path. If someone tells you they have credibility, chances are they don't. Let's look at some of the most powerful personal brands of all time. Martin Luther King, Jr. didn't tell people he was a great man who was selfless and had courage, he showed you. Gandhi didn't tell you he was a man of incredible mental strength, he showed you.

Researchers have found that if people have an initial negative experience with someone who creates a poor impression, they tend to avoid that person in the future. The challenge is that once an initial impression is set, it's very difficult to change that impression. You may need as many "at bats" or interactions with people as possible to change the impressions. Get more "at bats." When I coach executives, as an agent of the organization, it is my job to tell them how it is. Sometimes an impression is too deep, and the best thing a person can do is do something else. What I mean by this is sometimes people may need to leave an organization to become effective. Brands are powerful. Sometimes people are not willing to recognize or acknowledge progress and, when that happens, it's time to move on.

The bottom line when it comes to brand is we want people to be able to tell a story about us that makes a positive impression. If you want people to tell a positive story about you, find people you can tell a positive story about.

11

The Culture Culprit
Intentional Action

There are many organizational cultures that define the tone of companies. This tone is what reinforces or redirects what employees do and say. There are collaborative cultures, where employees work in collegial ways and have a team mentality. There are family-oriented cultures, where organizations value work-life balance in the hope that their employees will be more productive and satisfied with their corporate environment. However, there are also organizational cultures that erase productivity and motivation, such as when companies foster competitive environments or inconsistent expectations. These cultures can create a work environment that harbors resentment and feelings of hopelessness, often resulting in employees getting "stuck."

There are times when we all get stuck and that's okay. What's not okay is to stay stuck and blame it on the culture of your organization. Once you stay stuck you are perpetuating that culture and letting it dictate and override your behaviors. Yes, of course it's true that the culture of your organization plays a large role in your success or failure. However, they are not the only factors. The largest factor, and the one you have the most control over, is you and your belief system.

Simple Success Strategy: Intentional Action

When considering the various ways we make a decision, it's important to think of the many factors that shape and influence our behaviors. Similar to the multiple levels government agencies use to predict individuals' responses to crisis situations (The Social-Ecological Model, Center for Disease Control and Prevention, 2015), people respond to situations at work based on a variety of factors. The good news is once you know the factors, you can make progress.

Factor 1: You

The first consideration is how *you*, in general, tend to behave or respond. A large part of this aspect is determined by your personality. Although our personalities have the capacity to change and adapt across our lifespan (Nussbaum, 2015), we do have components of our disposition that are relatively stable and consistent. For example, think about a person, other than a family member, whom you would call in a crisis. You might have envisioned someone because they are reliable, and you know they'd answer and show up to help. Or, you could have selected someone because they get things done, and you know they'd figure out how to navigate hard situations. You could have even thought of someone because they are discreet, and you know you'd prefer whatever the crisis was to be handled with privacy. Whoever you thought of, you likely picked the person because of a specific trait that is important to you. They came to mind not just because they displayed that trait once, but likely because they demonstrated their reliability, ability to execute, or their discreetness, time and time again. It was a part of their disposition that is stable. Although we can most definitely change our behavioral norms across time, we have a tendency to react a certain way because of our personalities. This is important when considering how we respond to situations because it is known as our default—what we, in general, tend to do.

Factor 2: You, in a Context

Another factor that influences our behaviors is a context. We alter our dress, our tone, and our formalities depending on where we are and what role we are playing. We are going to interact with our families at a Sunday BBQ differently than how we interact at a Monday morning board meeting. We know we are expected to behave in certain ways in certain places, and we adjust our behaviors accordingly. Most of the time, these shifts in context or roles come naturally to us because we have taught ourselves with time to make them until they become habit. We often take safeguards to make sure we don't act out of context. I'll give you an example. I know someone who is more sarcastic and fun-natured around his friends. He easily and naturally makes the shift when he needs to at work, except when one of his clients is a friend. In that situation, this person makes sure that, no matter how informal the interaction is, he wears a tie. Why does he do this? To remind him of the professional context he is in. Although his friend teases and jokes with him out of work, he realizes that it might complicate the professional relationships with him and his colleagues if he doesn't switch roles when they are in a corporate setting. This example illustrates two things: 1) We are aware of context and take steps to make sure we act appropriately within them, and 2) We shift our behaviors depending on where we are or what role we are playing. This is important to remember because it impacts how you will respond at work. You might be very forthcoming in your personal life, but if you feel as though that trait isn't appropriate for the role you are playing at work, then you need to consider the smartest way to address that to get what you want in a situation.

Factor 3: You, in a Culture

The culture of an organization is powerful. If a company spends time building a positive culture, the payback can be enormous for both the leadership and those they hire. On the other hand, if the culture is negative, it can inhibit performance and motivation. This component builds on the first two factors because, regardless of how you normally act or how you act in a certain context, a culture can override those things in positive or negative ways. I know someone who is naturally opinionated and, regardless of context, often feels confident sharing her perspectives with others. However, when she started a new job she quickly realized that the culture was one where junior employees mostly listen to, and agree with, the senior employees. The organizational culture here was one of seniority, not expertise. She quickly felt frustrated because she felt she had two options: 1) Speak up and be labeled as disrespectful or 2) Be silent and not put her knowledge and training to use. Neither of these were good options to her because, whichever she chose, her expertise wasn't being heard. She quickly felt stuck because of her corporate culture.

You, In Action: Intentional Action

Intentional action is responding to a situation based on consideration of a variety of factors, which results in a strategy that enhances your chances of getting the outcome you desire. When faced with the need to take intentional action at work, especially when you feel stuck or limited, it is important to consider the role of all three factors (that is, you, the context, and the culture) when deciding how to act. The following are some decisions to make with regard to each of the factors.

Adjust Your Style into Strategy

The first step is to reflect on your behaviors and what is influencing them from each level: you, the context, and the culture. Are your behaviors your norm? If they aren't your norm, ask yourself why you're not using your most intuitive responses and consider if you should allow yourself to be "you." Most times the opposite will be the case, meaning that you are using your default personality traits and not trying a different approach. Behaviors and reactions can be classified as those that are part of your stable personality or disposition, such as a trait, or those that are more fleeting and temporal, such as state. An example relevant to the business world would be a conflict style. Let's say someone is avoidant by nature, so their conflict style is avoidant (trait). If that approach isn't allowing your voice to be heard or progress to be made, then you have to adjust your style into a strategy. For this particular goal, and for intentional action, you need to override your instincts of avoidance and strategize to be conflict-engaging (state). The similar idea applies to situations and cultures—are your expectations for the norms working? If not, how can you strategize so that you can intentionally act and overcome the obstacles of the situation or culture?

Assess the Change Potential

There are a range of reasons you will feel stuck at various points in your career and life. If adjusting your style into strategy, or reverting from a strategy back to your style, doesn't work then you have to consider the change potential. How much of an impact on this situation are you able to make, and how comfortable are you with that amount of change? If you make changes you are happy with by altering your individual tendencies and behaviors to align with those of the situation or culture, then the change potential can actually be quite large. You are either engaging in a way that helps you reframe the situation, such as realizing speaking up when you are naturally avoidant helps create policies you like, or people around you are responding to the behaviors in the ways you'd like. If you can help regain credibility in the work context by adapting the level of formality you use in e-mails and people are responding to that, then you are adequately adjusting to the context so the change potential is high.

Cultural changes are harder. Even though we know that people impact their environment, we also know that environment impacts people. Changing a culture takes time; however, people can make great strides with patience. If you compare and contrast a culture across a few months, you can consider the change potential by the level of openness with which the culture responded to the smaller alterations. For example, in one company the workers had to get travel expenses approved by five levels of supervisors. This took time and extra paperwork, and employees were frustrated with the red tape they had to go through to make mandatory work trips. Eventually, the company heard their disdain and adjusted the system to make it entirely online, which saved input time. It still took weeks for approval, but each entry was much less cumbersome and timely to initiate. That shows potential for change, even if it takes a while for the logistics to catch up.

Know When It's Not You, It's Them

After you've exhausted efforts on your end strategizing, reframing, and taking assessments of change, your intentional action might be to explore other options. At the end of the day, we can grow and adapt as individuals, but we need to see a response. If you have genuinely put the work in, do yourself a favor and know when the most strategic and intentional action would be to remove the negativity. That can mean you leave a company for another or, if it's your company, you make hard decisions and cut out the offending policy, people, or problem.

12

Political Denial
Be Savvy, Not Slimy

*A*n executive without political savvy is like a smartphone without a wireless carrier; you will have something to do, but you won't be connected to who and what you want.

Whether you like it or not, politics are part of business and life. In my experience, teaching political skills has been one of the hardest aspects of leadership development. This is not because the tools and techniques are hard to learn, but because of the baggage that the word "politics" bears. People do not like the idea of being political because it goes against their value system.

For good reason, the idea of being political or being involved with office politics creates a values conflict for people. This is completely understandable. People who have integrity do not want to play games or be thought of as a "brown noser." Influence, brand, and relationships are a big part of business. These are also political skills. You do not have to be "political" in order to have skills that help you excel within an organization. The way to think about this is being someone who has political savvy rather than being political. Your motivation for doing what you do is the difference. Someone who is political is someone who is primarily out for themselves. Someone who is ambitious as well as looks out for the organization and others has political savvy.

I was facilitating a panel for senior leaders. All of them were credible and smart people. However, one was a natural presenter and had strong presence. The other few on the panel were not as engaging or not as naturally strong storytellers. A common misstep I have seen people make is overshadowing a less charismatic person. This may be completely innocent, but it doesn't matter. The impact is that the other person will begin to have a negative view of you or think that you need to be a grand stander. In several instances, I have seen people not have the composure to refrain from telling another story or another funny anecdote. You may still nail it in the moment, but in the long term, it has a negative impact because people view it as your need to be in the spotlight. It sends a message that you don't have good judgment. I'm not suggesting being a wall flower, but what I am suggesting is you will get further by taking a back seat if you notice others around you need some help engaging others.

It's pretty clear what it looks like when someone is just out for themselves and is "political" for the purpose of being solely self-serving. We have plenty of examples of people in the business and political world who are full of double talk and lack integrity. There are also people who get ahead because they are extraordinary at treating people above them very well, but treating people below them poorly. It's my belief that you are only as strong as your foundation. If you build yourself on fragmented relationships, people will be happy to be the crack in the concrete that makes your foundation weak and leaky. This means that if you don't treat people well regardless of where they are in the organization, it will come back to bite you at some point.

Simple Success Strategy: Be Savvy, Not Slimy

Just getting your work done, doesn't get it done. I've witnessed the unfortunate causalities of people who won't engage in the work inside of the work. What I mean by this is that there is work to be done that is outside of your core function. For example, a person who is a software engineer can do well if he/she just keeps their head down and delivers. However, the software engineer who builds relationships outside their work team and provides a point of view in meetings will have more upward mobility and accelerate their upward progression more quickly. How do I know this? I know this because I am frequently a part of the conversations when executives are deciding who to promote and why or why not.

The people who are most successful navigating the game of politics of business are the ones who are genuine.

They come across as authentic, transparent, and not trying to be political. The key is to have political skill and will so you can leverage your influence for your advancement and the benefit of the business and others around you.

The more effective you are at demonstrating political savvy, the more effective you can be at advocating for others. If you have people who work for you, there is no doubt that they are more motivated and engaged if they believe in your ability to influence upward. Having strong political savvy allows you to build relationship capital. Relationship capital works just like cash. The more relationship capital you have, the more you can invest in people and the more people will invest in you because you are perceived to have value. People with political savvy have strong insight into how decisions are made and who to talk to when it matters. If you have political savvy, you are also less likely to be caught off guard when changes happen in the organization.

It all starts with comfort and willingness. Whatever you need to do to reframe the importance of developing political skill, do it. You may not be the most natural at networking and building relationships. That's okay. Find the people you are aligned with who you can associate with. Keep these relationships close and they will help you help yourself.

Create a Political Promoter Profile

In order to get ahead, you need to be thinking ahead. In Frank Reichheld and Rob Markey's (2011) work, they talk about the importance of a net promoter score. This philosophy has been used to assess customer relationships as well as look at manager and subordinate relationships. The basic philosophy is that you want to know whether people or companies would be likely to recommend you or your work or would actively advise against working with your or your service. People support companies and people they admire and believe in. People willingly advocate for people they believe in or actively get in the way of people they don't believe in. Just like you would take a strategic approach to getting your work done, take a strategic approach to developing a political promoter profile. Identify people within and outside your organization who can help or hurt you. There are three types of people as it relates to a political promoter profile. Depending on what category they fall in, you either need to leverage their beliefs about you or repair relationships. The three categories are: promoters, neutral, or opponents.

Promoter: A person who actively advances your advancement in any way.

Neutral: A person who is neutral related to your advancement.

Opponent: A person who intentionally holds back your advancement.

You don't need everyone to be a promoter, but if you have people who are opponents and they have positional power (superior to you in the organization) and a high probability of taking action (influential), then it's important that you get on their good side and at least get them to neutral. It's a pretty simple equation. The more people you have as "promoters" and the less people you have as "opponents," the better positioned you will be politically.

Sharpen your Signature Strengths

The sharper your strengths are, the more people remember you for what you can do rather than what you can't do. A benefit of this approach is that most people enjoy what they are good at and the journey will keep you motivated and engaged. Instead of just focusing on areas of growth, find something you are good at and get better. This doesn't mean you don't address potential career deal breakers like having emotional outbursts or lacking fairness. It does mean that it is beneficial to hedge your bets at knowing what you are good at and getting even better. I have seen that people advance faster within their careers when they are known for their signature strengths and continue to develop them and bring along others.

Whether or not you are comfortable with the political aspect of business and life, it is a large predictor of success. You can maintain your values and still demonstrate skills that will help you get ahead without intentionally leaving others behind.

13

Ignoring Your Intuition

Judge a Book by its Cover

We judge ourselves on intent and others on impact. One example I can give you is thinking about one of your recent driving experiences. I grew up in Northern New Jersey, a place full of fast drivers who need to get everywhere five minutes ago for no particular reason. If you are driving somewhere and a person cuts you off, what do you think about that person? That's right, it often involves a certain nonverbal symbol common in New Jersey. What about when you are in a rush to get to an important meeting and you realize you need to get to the exit and there is someone to your right? Then you speed up a bit and move over so you can catch your exit. What do you think about yourself? What do you think the person behind you thinks of you? It's natural and it's okay.

We take a slice of time, an instance, one behavior, and make judgments about other people. However, when it comes to us, we expect people to know what our intentions were. What's the point? Keep this in mind and know that it's natural that people will make snap judgments about us and us about others. Although it's important to know about snap judgments we make and how they can be wrong, it is also important to know that they serve a purpose and can also be right.

As long as we are aware of how our intuition works and it works fast, it is okay to use this information to our advantage. The idea of unconscious bias has been a large part of discussion and has gotten much media attention. There is a lot of truth in the thought that we all have biases and we make decisions based on these biases. At times, this seems to be automatic and we aren't even aware it's happening, so it can be a challenge. This means that you think something about someone that isn't true, just because of your unconscious bias. It's absolutely critical to success and being a good human being that we are aware of our biases and how they impact our decisions and behaviors.

With that being said, and I realize this is controversial, I believe it has gone too far. I see too many people questioning their intuition and gut for fear of being labeled. People question one of their greatest gifts of being a human, and that's intuition. Intuition has a lot of power and tells us something. The keys are awareness and maturity. You need to be aware of how your biases are impacting you and be mature enough to use them rather than letting them use you.

Your values will also impact your judgments. It's important to know what your values are, because when something is out of alignment with your values you can make snap judgments. Now let's talk about what to do in order to leverage your intuition rather than ignore it.

Simple Success Strategy: Judge a Book by its Cover

Learn to go with your gut, it always goes with you. You will read or hear this from me in many contexts. Leverage what you have and what your intuition is telling you. Use it as a data point; just don't use it as the only data point. When I say "judge a book by its cover," what I am referring to is the art of seeing something and what it is saying to you. For example, let's say you see two people at a restaurant having a candle lit dinner and holding hands. One of them is staring into the other person's eyes and rubbing the other person's hand. The other person is consistently looking over the other person's shoulder and making eye contact with someone else and smiling with someone who is sitting at the bar. Sure, the person making eye contact with those other than the person they are with could be a fashion designer who specializes in tight clothing, but my read would be that this person is more interested in someone other than the person they are with. Certainly, there could be a host of reasons for the behavior that you just aren't aware of.

My point is this: in my experience, in the overwhelming majority of situations, my instinct and the instinct of the people I advise has been on target. That little feeling you get, that vibe, it is data. It's not the only data, but it is data and data you want to pay attention to if you want to be successful.

I believe we all have *reaction radar.* Just like any radar, our reaction radar can be turned on or turned off. We can spend time and effort to upgrade the capability of our reaction radar or just leave it alone. Our reaction radar can be used to make decisions, or it can be ignored. We have the human technology to make predictions based on our instincts; my advice is to use it, and continue to update its software.

I spent a year getting trained in group therapy. For six months I wasn't allowed to speak, just observe. All I was permitted to do was to take notes on behavior. It was process observation at its truest level. No judgments, just behaviors. It taught me that, very often, people are not aware of the messages that they send to others and how frequently people misperceive what others are communicating. For example, there was a participant in the group who would often cross her arms during the sessions. People took it personally and perceived her crossing her arms as a way of communicating that she was uninterested or closed off. In reality, it was simply because she often got cold in the room.

Therefore, I completely get that there is often a gap between intention and impact. More times than not, an impression is spot on and you should not deny yourself the use of that gut instinct. At the same time, you want to have a fast and practical process to keep yourself honest and not just make snap judgments. The bottom line is it's about balance. The following process will help you judge a book by its cover so you can decide if you need to read more or if you can keep it closed.

Read

What do you see and what does what you see tell you? This is the judgment zone. Let your bias come out, but keep it to yourself for now. Don't act. Just be aware. What are you saying to yourself? What judgments are you making? What do you think is going on? What are you experiencing? Is it an intense or subtle feeling? If you had one guess as to what was happening and why, what would it be?

Reset

Now, hit the reset button and take a step back. This is where you temporarily remove your initial reaction. Take the judgment out and see the person and situation from as many different perspectives as you can. The easiest practice is to have a few people in mind who think very differently from you. For example, I have a close friend who is an accountant and is very analytical, a friend who is a salesperson and is very social, a friend who is a counselor and very understanding, and a friend who is a banker and is very results-driven. The point is to integrate other possible perspectives.

Respond

Once you know what your initial reaction was, why, and thought through multiple perspectives, you can make a strategic response. This means you can make a decision and respond and take action with an informed mindset. This is about being strategic rather than reactive and moving forward with your assessment with confidence.

As I mentioned previously, I know that this is a controversial topic, and of course I have been wrong. I do believe that instincts come from experiences and that those experiences should be leveraged. Although some will cite examples of how people's biases and initial reactions are wrong, I would argue that it is right many more times than it is wrong. All I advise is that you become aware and take action based on your awareness. Use that reaction radar and set your direction. Your initial judgment might be right or it might be wrong, but at least you can use it rather than lose it.

Section 3

Leading

14

Innovation Evaporation
Innovation Creation

Innovation is just a word, but it is a word that is polarizing. It either excites or scares people. It can put pressure on people and businesses to always be the first and the fastest, and it can consume energy. However, if you think of innovation in a limited way, such as discovering something cutting edge or technologically savvy, then you are missing the point. The point of innovation is to have vision for emerging changes, and then be committed to responding to change in smart ways.

Innovation is about seeing things differently, so you have the opportunity to do things differently. When people think about innovation, they tend to think of it as more of a revolution, like the creation of the iPhone.

Though the iPhone is brilliant and changed the way people communicate, operate, and live, not every innovation has to be earth-shattering.

The trap people typically fall into is saying to themselves, "It's the way we've always done things." As complex as our minds are, they are also simple. Once we write a script, our minds like to stick with it, similar to a code in software development. If "it's the way we've always done things" is your typical reaction, you need to ramp up on the innovation.

One of the most disheartening consequences of the Great Recession is that businesses and people are scared. There is so much focus on fear that it not only impacts productivity, it hinders creativity. With my clients prior to 2008, risk was rewarded. Granted, that was part of the problem. There was too much risk in certain industries. However, I believe there has been an overcorrection, so much so that people are rewarded and reinforced for saying "no" more than they are for saying "yes." It simply has made it harder for companies to innovate and progress. Even worse, it has had an impact on individuals because they are fearful of making the wrong decisions at the wrong time and getting punished.

One company I worked with was so risk averse that the employees used to call the decision-making process "the slow no." Now, of course, calculated risk management is critical to success, but not at the expense of a work environment where people feel like they are constantly standing still. Staying comfortable is pretty comfortable—until something changes, and the odds of something changing are pretty good.

Simple Success Strategy: Innovation Creation

Being disruptive in a positive way is a theme for many of the clients I work with. The idea is to rock the boat just enough to get people thinking differently, or innovatively, but not so much that you lose focus of your direction and sink the ship. Being disruptive in a positive way is about creating space for people to think differently without repercussion. There are three phases in getting started on innovation: contemplation, concentration, and creation.

Contemplation

Contemplation is when you start to ask yourself questions about the status quo. It is both an emotional and logical process. In the contemplation phase, you are negotiating with yourself on if and how to move forward.

Let's set up a simple decision flow chart. The way this works is simple. Depending on what your answer is to the first question, you either move on to the next step or you stand still.

1. Are you unhappy or frustrated with the way things are going?
   a. If no, congratulations and enjoy.
   b. If yes, go to the next question.
2. Do you have the courage to do something differently?
   a. If no, see question 1.
   b. If yes, go to question 3.

3. Do you have the capability to do something differently?
   a. If no, identify what you need and who can help you get started.
   b. If yes, start by taking your first step today.

Concentration

Shift. Sometimes you just need to make the shift from contemplation to concentration. You made the decision that you are moving toward something else. This is where you plan and focus what you could do differently. Concentration is about focus.

Here are the five whats of concentration:

1. What if?
2. What can get in the way?
3. What will help me get there?
4. What will I do today?
5. What do I need from others?

Creation

Here, there is no thinking, no parameters, just open-minded creating. The best way to get into a creation mindset is to set aside a period of time, let's say two hours a month. In Daniel Pink's TED Talk called "Drive," he describes a company that gives its employees a certain amount of time to innovate. All they need to do is to share their innovation with the group in a fun meeting. With time, groups have come up with great and beneficial innovations that they might have missed had they not been encouraged to spend time simply creating.

Trust me, in my work with financial institutions on Wall Street, I have heard every reason why this approach can't work. I understand that you can't give people half a day each week to "be innovative." However, could you give yourself a half hour a month to focus on innovation or thinking about what could be better if you had no parameters? What about presenting the idea to people you work with and seeing if you could allow for a half hour a month to focus on innovation? Think about how devoting that time now could allow you to be proactive or innovative, rather than reactive. Reactivity often consumes much more time and has far more limited options.

Creating an Atmosphere for Innovation

One of the biggest challenges people have related to innovation at work is that it isn't welcomed. If you are a boss, you have a tremendous opportunity to make that cultural shift. If you are all in and want to be a leader who creates a culture of innovation, there are a few things to pay attention to: space and pace. Space is setting up the rules and guidelines, such as having a process for how all ideas are given a chance. One strategy is creating a basic high-level template for idea creation. People put down some big-picture ideas and answer a few questions. Then, you can have people present others' ideas at random so there is not bias based on personal relationships or positional power.

Pace is about how slowly or quickly you move through ideas, debate, and conversations. I'm personally a fan of fast. However, I realize that sometimes it pays off to take time to let ideas evolve. What you can do here is vary the time and pace of conversations around innovation. I would also suggest giving people time outside of a group discussion to think through their ideas by providing them with a few points to think about ahead of time. With this approach, you take advantage of those people who like to think and innovate in the moment and those who like to have some time to prepare.

Let me be clear: It is okay to not innovate. Sometimes, staying with the status quo works. The reason innovation, whether it is new product development or professional development, is critical is that people and technology around you are moving fast. If they are moving fast and forward, well, that puts you going in reverse, which is why the focus is on innovation creation to prevent innovation evaporation.

15

Motivation Complication
Pay People with Their Motivational Currency

M otivation. It's a word that has taken on new meaning and stronger importance as companies strive to get the best out of people in a game where the rules have changed. Prior to 2008, when the financial crisis set in, the main motivation was financial rewards or promotions. Now there are more regulations, more options for emerging talent, and less cash to go around. That's the bad news. The good news is that companies are more committed than ever to find ways to motivate their people.

No matter what the industry, no matter what the role, people struggle with motivating themselves and motivating others. It's consistently a top area of concern for businesses. Since the Great Recession, businesses have been struggling to get people to do more with less. They all want a silver bullet to motivate people. Well, as I'm sure you already know, there is no one fix for all. However, that's not necessarily bad news.

Think about when someone takes the time to remember your name and get to know you as an individual. In my experience, there is a strong correlation between learning and remembering someone's name and the probability of engaging them. This mundane habit is often a catalyst for learning more about what a person cares about or prioritizes. As with most of my advice, it's pretty simple. Get to know people and what they care about and leverage that. Too often, leaders make the mistake of focusing on their own greatest skill or motivator. For example, if a leader is results- and numbers-driven, he or she will try to motivate using results and numbers. Sounds like a good strategy, right? Wrong. It's terrible. People don't want to be led according to what motivates you; they want to be led according to what motivates them.

How do we figure this out? First we need to know what we are looking for, and then we need to adapt to capitalize on it.

Simple Success Strategy: Pay People with Their Motivational Currency

If you don't know where individuals want to go, how can you point them in the correct direction? The goal is to leverage what motivates people so they are engaged and want to take action. Ask yourself, have you ever had someone do something you needed done without asking for it? That's called initiative or discretionary effort. People want to do things, and they want to do them well. As a leader you just need to tap into their *motivational currency*.

How do we know what motivates people and, just as important, what do we do once we know? Harvard professor David McClelland's (1961) research on motivation identifies three social motives: achievement, affiliation, and power. The theory is that these three motives move people toward behavior. Modifying his theoretical framework and combining it with more than a decade of my own experiences working with companies, I developed the *Motivational Currency Calculator* (MCC) (*Calculating Your Motivational Currency Blog*, Fazio, 2015). This resource is a direct, simple approach to identifying and leveraging individuals' motivational currency.

Motivational Currency Calculator: The Core Four

In my view, many things drive people. However, for the most part, they fall into four basic areas: performance, people, power, and purpose. The most skilled leaders recognize that motivations come in a variety of currencies, and learning the process of converting those currencies is the key to moving people to action. Drawing from theoretical research that helps us understand how people are motivated, this MCC gives you an accessible and straightforward way to leverage this knowledge into your business domain.

As much as we wish it were as simple as a one size fits all, when it comes to motivation and much of psychology, people are unique, and we take action based on our personalities, previous experiences, and current situation. What this means is that although most people will have a primary motivator, it is often the case that people have multiple motivators. Someone can be highly motivated by more than one driver at a time. Someone could be just as driven by performance as they are by people. The stronger your motivators are in one area, the easier it is for you to make decisions and the more challenging it is to manage your impulses.

The following are descriptions of the four motivators, presented in an intuitive and straightforward way. The goals are to be able to: a) Identify what your primary motivators are, b) Read what the motivators are for others, and c) Lead with intention so you can motivate others quickly and effectively.

Performance. The performance motivator is about results. Individuals who are driven by performance want to get things done. They pride themselves on not just completing tasks, but excelling. A person with a drive for performance thrives on meeting challenges and exceeding standards. They are often fast-paced, direct, and focused on outcomes. Performance-driven people are not afraid to challenge the status quo and expect others to have as much drive as they do.

A potential setback for individuals who are performance-driven is overlooking the impact getting tasks completed has on other people. If someone is extremely motivated by performance, they have a tendency to focus on the outcome and not pay a lot of attention to the process. They can be perceived as overly direct or controlling.

In groups, the performance-driven person is often the person who takes the lead and drives things to resolution. They can come across as controlling or demanding. They want to drive to resolution and complete a task or set a new standard.

People. The people motivator is about relationships. Individuals who are driven by the people motivator are most concerned about getting along, teamwork, and collaboration. They are focused on how things impact others. They tend to have strong social radar and can read people well.

A potential setback for individuals who are people-driven is they can lose sight of an objective because they are overly concerned on how others feel. If someone is overly people-focused, they can get caught up in the process and not pay attention to the result. They can be perceived as too feelings-oriented or indirect.

In groups, the people-driven person is often the one who asks a lot of questions, is inclusive, and focuses on getting everyone's opinion. A common descriptor of someone who is people-driven is "nice" or "team-oriented."

Power. The power motivator is about influence. People who are motivated by power put a premium on being persuasive and offering their point of view. They often are effective at providing advice and communicating the importance of brand and reputation.

A potential setback for individuals who are power-driven is they get caught up in status and reputation. They have a need to feel important and receive recognition. They can come across as "one uppers," meaning people who tend to build on what other people say and highlight their experience. They can be perceived as insecure if they have not reached the academic or professional status of those around them.

In groups, the power-driven person is often the person who gives their point of view early and often. Power-driven people have a desire to be influential, so they often tell stories and talk about the big picture or how things "will be." They often give unsolicited advice. They have a tendency to hint or overtly communicate who they know and how important they are.

Purpose. The purpose motivator is about helping others and contributing to something outside of themselves. They often crave having purpose and meaning in their work. Many purpose-driven people are motivated by developing others or volunteering and community involvement. They excel at getting people to focus on the greater good and can be tremendous enterprise contributors. They can get people to think across business silos and think about what is best for the entire group or business rather than individuals or teams.

A potential setback for individuals who are purpose-driven is they can become disengaged if there is no meaning or a focus on the greater good in their work. They have a need to see the bigger picture and are passionate about being selfless. They often focus on learning about businesses, cultures, or communities outside of their own. They often are eager to find resources that will help them help others.

In groups, a purpose-driven person tends to try to find ways to connect what they are doing to a bigger picture. They will often question the purpose of an initiative.

They can be perceived as overly idealistic or not focused on identified results. A common stereotype, right or wrong, of Millennials is that they are purpose-driven.

Awareness and action are cornerstones of progress and success. If you want a more in-depth understanding of your motivational currency profile and how you can be more effective at motivating others, you can contact us at Info@OnPointAdvising.com to take the Motivational Currency Calculator (MCC). This will give you insights into what your key motivators are and how to assess and align with motivators in others.

Although motivation can seem abstract and complicated, there are some simple strategies that yield results. The mistake I see many managers making is treating motivation as something that they need to do to employees, rather than something that leaders do with employees. There is no one-size-fits-all silver bullet. However, there are strategies that work. It starts with a motivation mindset and ends with being intentional about knowing what makes you and others tick so you spend your time wisely and help others do the same.

When people talk about motivation, they usually talk about it from the perspective of "how do I motivate

Motivational Currency Calculator Overview

Performance	People	Power	Purpose
Results	Relationships	Influence	Helping Others
Achievment	Teamwork	Persuasion	Contributing to "Something Greater"
Challenge	Collaboration	Selling	Meaning
Goals	Harmony	Advising	Community Impact

© Rob Fazio, PhD, OnPoint Advising, Inc.

others"? I have been extremely fortunate during the past several years to learn from Howard Ross, who is a partner at LLR Partners, a private equity firm in Philadelphia. Quite simply put, Howard is as helpful as he is brilliant. I asked him the question, "What is the most helpful yet simple strategy you could offer people?" He said to stay focused on your core business and your business needs. He went on to explain that too often people let their personal needs get in the way of their business needs. His example was that he often sees CEOs and entrepreneurs making the mistake of straying away from what they do best or buying a huge building because of ego or trying to prove something. He added that if you can't manage it yourself, turn over the business to someone who can grow it effectively and exercise your dreams or needs in another context.

Howard's simple strategy magnifies the importance of knowing what your own motivational currency is. If you are someone who is extremely high in power and low in all the other areas, there is a chance that you could lose focus on what you need to do to follow through on your core business needs. The point is to be able to recognize your tendencies so you don't make poor decisions solely based on your personal needs.

16

Passive Persuasion
The Persuasion Pyramid

Your ability to persuade will have a direct impact on how effective you are at getting what you want when you want. Persuasion is a skill, just like writing a report. It's a big part of success and if you don't develop this skill, others will, and you will always be persuaded as opposed to the one persuading. When you take a passive approach to persuasion you leave too much up to chance and your probability of success decreases.

Persuading and influencing others is not something that comes naturally to all people. Whether persuasion comes naturally to you or not is less important than the fact that you can develop a strong ability to persuade if you want. Let's start with a major challenge that I see many people have when they want to be persuasive and fail. I call it *finishing before you start.* This is when people have already convinced themselves that they won't be able to persuade someone to their point of view. They make their feelings into facts, rather than just a data point.

For example, I was working with an executive, let's call him Steve, who always gave up before he tried. He wanted to demonstrate to his boss that there was a better way to approach the way they were working. When we initially started talking about how he could influence his boss, his first response was, "My boss will never go for this." My client was absolutely convinced that no matter what, his boss would shoot him down and his point of view wasn't worth raising. Once Steve convinced himself his boss wasn't going to value his opinion, he was finished before he started. Steve set himself up for failure. His thought process, nonverbal messages, and beliefs all followed what he told himself.

I knew we needed to change the narrative from Steve knowing he *wasn't* going to be successful in influencing, to knowing he *was* going to be successful. After years of coaching executives and athletes I've learned it's not always about intellect and logic, but about something else. So we needed to find a way for Steve to go from *finishing before he started* to *starting before he finished.* In other words, Steve needed to give himself a chance and it started with his mindset.

Simple Success Strategy: The Persuasion Pyramid

So, what did we do? We started with the three core aspects of successful persuasion: confidence, competence, and comfort. I call this the Persuasion Pyramid. You can get by if you have one without the other, but you need all three to be successful at influencing on a consistent basis. Confidence is your belief that you can influence someone or a group of people. Competence is having the skills to be influential. Comfort is being okay over being empowered and influential. Just because you are effective at persuading, doesn't necessarily mean you are doing anything wrong or taking advantage of someone. Actually, the opposite is true, the more persuasive you are, the more you can help others help themselves.

When you are able to diagnose in which area your challenges typically lay, you can do something to be more effective. The following is a snapshot of the three core areas of the Persuasion Pyramid.

The Persuasion Pyramid will help you become aware of where you need to focus. Persuasion starts with yourself. The more confidence you have, the more comfortable you will be and the higher your probability of successful influence will be. Each of the following characteristics, being calculated, credible, and concise, will help you gain confidence, competence, and comfort with time. Focus on developing them and you will see your capability grow.

Calculated

The more intentional and strategic you are, the better able you will be to respond in the moment. Think through what the other person is likely to say and how they will react. Identify what topics may come up that could throw you off your focus. Know what you want prior

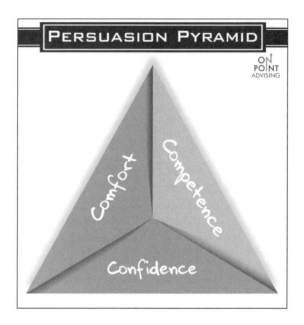

to the conversation. It is also very beneficial to know what the other person's motivational currency is (Chapter 15) and which conversation character (Chapter 20) he or she is aligned with.

Credible

The notion of credibility has been researched and popularized by two thought leaders in the leadership space, Kouzes and Posner (2003). They wrote the book on credibility: *Credibility: How Leaders Gain and Lose It, Why People Demand It*. What I have learned from their work, as well as working with executives, is that there is a pretty simple equation related to credibility and persuasion. The more credible you are, the easier it is for you to persuade

Persuasion Pyramid Description

	Description	Example
Confidence	Belief in your ability.	Knowing you can successfully influence someone.
Competence	Skills that help you influence.	Reading a situation and a person so you know what is important to them.
Comfort	Level of ease you feel.	Coaching and convincing yourself that you have a right to persuade and influence. Not letting yourself get in the way of your successful influencing.

people. The people around you determine your credibility. They determine this by what you say and what you do. The good news is that you can influence your credibility. Some of the key building blocks of credibility are transparent communication, following through on commitments, managing your emotions, and treating people with respect. People also view leaders as credible when they are visionary and demonstrate the confidence and conviction to make a decision or give an unpopular point of view. It takes a lot of time to build your credibility and very little time to deplete it. Do you know anyone who wants to work for someone whom they can't trust?

Concise

As I am confident you have already heard, communication is a key factor in whether or not we are effective. I was coaching an executive who was very gifted in the technology space. He was brilliant, but could not break his habit of being overly verbose. His communication style was the biggest barrier to success. People would tune him out as soon as he started talking because they knew he was going to be long-winded.

People are busy; they want information fast and in a concise manner. Many people get caught up in wanting to showcase how much time they spent uncovering information and research. The point is, though, how long it took you to add value is irrelevant—it's how effectively you can deliver value that is relevant.

A way to increase your chances of being an effective and concise communicator is to follow a simple framework: *overview, review,* and *point of view.* Overview is the headline, a way to let the person know where you are going. It's brief and catches the person's attention. Review is a snapshot of 3–5 key points. Think of them as bullet points that support your overview. Point of view is the bottom line. It's your recommendation, suggestion, or even key question that you have. It's where you land. This type of communication forces you to synthesize and think through what is most relevant.

This type of communication can be used in one-on-one conversations, presentations, and e-mails. Again, you can always provide more detailed information. Your ability to master this style of communication will greatly increase your chances of being viewed as credible and a valuable contributor.

We cannot control what others do and decide. However, we can have a great deal of influence on what people do and decide. I'm not suggesting that you want to be pushing people around, but I am suggesting that you want to be really good at getting people to see different things in different ways, and you will want to do the same for others.

17

Analysis Paralysis
Decision Precision

" If you choose not to decide, you still have made a choice."

These lyrics from Rush's famous song "Freewill" has a lot of wisdom. Waiting is not deciding. Thinking is helpful, but overthinking is wasteful. The best leaders are people who think enough to make an informed decision and take action. We are all bombarded with information and overwhelmed with newsfeeds and data. It's not that information isn't helpful—it is—but if you only focus on inputs, you may not get to the output.

Calculated speed is a sign of confidence, intelligence, and effectiveness. I say calculated speed, because it's not just about doing things. It is, however, about getting the right things done in a timely manner. People actually respect others more when they make a wrong decision and grow from it as opposed to those who are afraid to make decisions.

Some people are naturally confident and comfortable with making decisions. For others, making a decision is a thorn in their side and they procrastinate until the decision is made for them. Decision-making is just a skill. By definition, a skill is something that can be learned. I believe that people who think they aren't good at making decisions have talked themselves out of being effective at it. A lot of the work I do with executives is around credibility. One of the quickest ways to lose or gain credibility is around decision-making. If you are thought of as someone who can't make a decision, it detracts from your credibility bank account; and if you are thought of as someone who can make tough decisions, it makes deposits in your credibility bank account.

Just as in the development of any skill, there are common mistakes and missteps that people can make. The following are some of the most common challenges and mistakes that people make when making decisions.

1. Thinking that the more important a decision is, the more difficult it has to be to make one.
2. Believing that the amount of time you spend on a decision directly improves its value.
3. Spending too much time on collecting more information than you need.
4. Letting feelings cripple your progress.
5. Going with your first choice.

6. Worrying too much about what others think.
7. Not worrying at all about what others think.
8. Not having a consistent approach to making a decision.

There are a variety of approaches to making a decision. It's critical to know up front which approach you are taking. In the spirit of keeping it simple, let's put them into three buckets: command, consensus, and combination. A command decision is when there is one person in control and he/she is making the decision, period. It's often the case that the decision has already been made and there is no need to involve others in the process. A consensus decision is an approach where all parties involved make the decision. The goal is to get all points of view and make a decision that everyone can support. A combination decision is when you integrate the points of views of others, and then either make the decision on your own or designate someone or some group of people to make the decision.

I asked someone who makes many decisions daily what their most helpful, yet simple success strategy is. Khadijah Sharif-Drinkard who is Vice President and Associate General Counsel at BET Networks (A Viacom Company), offered clear advice. Her message was to get the work done, even if there is chaos. She explained that you don't have as much influence going forward when you make decisions if you don't have a record of delivering. Her simple success strategy is clear and offers insight on how the decision to "get the work done" leads to credibility.

Simple Success Strategy: Decision Precision

If you are the decision-maker, own that role. If you already have a decision made or aren't going to integrate the points of view from other people, don't waste their time. It's also okay to let people know that you want their input, but will make the final decision. Clarity is king. As long as you are clear up front, you will be setting yourself up for success. Having an approach to making decisions and having confidence in that approach works. Now that we have focused on where people make mistakes, let's focus on what works and works fast. Decision precision includes three steps: define, deliberate, and decide.

Define

In this step, the focus is on defining the challenge and defining the decision rules. During this step, you think through how important and how urgent the decision is. This is where you give yourself a timeline and decide who needs to be involved in making the decision. When determining who should be involved in the decision process, be strategic and think through it from two perspectives, practical and political. The practical is about who has information or expertise that you can leverage. The political is about who needs to be involved or informed so you don't alienate anyone. You can use this as an opportunity to build alliances.

Deliberate

In this step, the focus is on identifying the range of options. During this process, you can make a list of the possible outcomes and their impact. It's also an opportunity to discuss the potential options with others. You should make it a priority to get as many viewpoints from as many people as possible. Whether you get diverse viewpoints from other people or you think it through yourself, you need to include three core approaches. It's likely that you tend to see things and make decisions based on one of three mindsets: *head, heart,* and *hands.*

The *head* mindset is all about being analytical and logical. When you see things through this mindset, you are focused on the rational side of things and the facts. Your primary concern is around getting things right and ensuring you focused on the right things.

The *heart* mindset is all about dealing with feeling. When you see things through this mindset, you are focused on emotion and how decisions impact others. The primary concern is on how the decision you make will make others feel.

The *hands* mindset is all about getting things done. When you see things through this mindset, you are focused on how quickly you can take action. The primary concern is on results and moving on to the next action item.

Each of these mindsets is valuable and plays a role. During the deliberation phase, it's important to pay attention to all three of these mindsets. Identify which one of the three you tend to align with. Protect yourself from making decisions that you only see through your point of view or primary mindset. The best thing you can do is to identify people who have different mindsets and talk through your decisions from their point of view.

Decide

Make the decision and move forward with confidence. Have confidence in the process and that you have spent the time to do your due diligence. The hardest thing about making a decision is struggling before the decision is made. The greatest thing about making a decision is that, once it's decided, it's done.

Forward motion is our intention and our focus. That doesn't mean that you can't get stuck or have bad days when you are moving slow. It just means that you need to be accountable to yourself to not staying stuck and let yourself get into a "what if" whirlpool of spiraling thoughts. If you are someone who tends to overthink things, find people and approaches that get you out of the analysis and into the action.

18

The Lone Ranger
Embrace the Stranger Danger

The one common factor that all successful people have is people. It's that simple. People are the core component of how to get to where you want to go. Think about it. Other people are the resource that can accelerate your ascent toward success or accelerate your decline. Most of us know that people are important, but it's evident to me that people aren't as strategic with their relationships as they are with other parts of their careers.

For some, building and leveraging relationships comes naturally. To others, it is a challenge. Regardless if it's easy or not, you need to consistently be building a network to ensure success, as well as create an insurance policy for the future. Many people who are results-focused overlook the value of relationships. If you move too fast, you can sacrifice an opportunity to deepen a relationship that will pay you dividends down the road. If you are someone who has reached your goals and enjoyed success, but have not thought of others, now is the time to start.

In my psychology training, I always thought characterizing people as "extroverts" or "introverts" was an over simplification of a more complex makeup of people. There are plenty of people who draw energy from others, but get hyper-focused on a goal and discount relationships in the process. There are also people who need time to recharge by taking time to themselves but are extremely socially gifted. The point is, whether you enjoy building relationships or not, you need to do it if you want to get what you want in the long term.

Relationships are anything but black and white. They are grey. There is always give and take in relationships and they are not always easy, but they are critical. They're so critical that if you don't have them, you will miss out on opportunities in life and promotions in your career.

Simple Success Strategy: Embrace the Stranger Danger

The best thing you can do in life is share it with others. Though that sounds soft and mushy, let me play this out for you. Researchers Van Boven and Gilovich (2003) have found that if you want to be happy, invest in experiences, not things. Intentionally create memories and moments with people. These experiences—more than things—have an impact and promote lasting positive feelings. The researchers found that experiences are a stronger predictor of happiness because they are open to positive interpretations, include meaning, and have a positive impact on successful relationships.

How does this relate to the importance of relationships? Relationships lead to results and revenue. The results and/or revenue do not have to be just in a financial sense. The results can be opportunities and positive experiences. If you make the effort to develop relationships, you increase the probability of creating experiences where people get to know you and that increases the chances that people want to collaborate and succeed together.

An approach that has served many of my clients well is to find your "relationship rock star." Some people are just naturally good at building relationships and connecting people. Adam Berman, who is the head of Talent at TayganPoint Consulting Group, is one of the best in the business. Why is he one of the best? He is a connector. What separates him from other connectors is that he only connects "A" players. This means that he doesn't waste people's time. A common mistake related to networking is that people connect anyone with everyone. With time, people in your network become less willing to meet with people you suggest. This is different from asking someone to do a favor and meeting with someone who is looking for guidance or support. Helping people by connecting them with others can be smart, but you don't want to burden people.

Lean Into Your Discomfort

Some of the best advice I got as I was sharpening my executive coaching skills came from a former colleague, Rich

Silvestri. Rich would take the time to talk with me about how to approach work with the most senior of executives as well as my business development skills. Rich keyed in on something that was incredibly helpful to me in my career and life. His advice was for me to "lean into my discomfort." It was actually completely aligned with who I strive to be, which is someone who takes challenges head on and, if need be, goes toward the storm. What's the point? Whether you are aware of it or not, we all have things that make us uncomfortable and they can be holding you back. Find out what they are and move toward them.

Build Relationship Capital

The idea of building capital when it comes to money is common sense. The idea is that, with time, you need to consistently build up your funds so you have cash in reserve to take action on a good deal or save you when times are tough. We've all heard that it is financially smart to keep 6–12 months of funding in reserve in case there is a downturn or an opportunity. The adage "cash is king" applies to relationships as well. Relationship capital is king. Building relationships before you need them is one of the most strategic and beneficial things you can do to propel your success. I take a three-point approach to building relationship capital. The philosophy is that the more relationship capital you build, the more you can accomplish for yourself and others.

Find, foster, and fix. The process includes three actions: find, foster, and fix. *Find* includes developing new relationships and intentionally reaching out to people you do not currently have relationships with inside and outside your organization. *Foster* is about taking your relationships to another level. This is about getting to know people in different ways. If you can genuinely identify ways to play a role in each other's ambitions, you will set yourself on a positive path of growth. *Fix* involves repairing any relationships that have been strained in any way. A major setback for people is having several people they know that for some reason they do not have a strong relationship with. They may have a negative view of something you did, or even misinterpreted something that happened along the way, or one of you may have made a mistake. You don't need to have a buddy-buddy relationship with everyone, but you do want to get to a place where there is at least mutual respect. You don't want to have people out there who you have poor relationships with who will actively hold you back or who you may need help from down the line.

These three actions can be accomplished by simple efforts such as grabbing a coffee, lunch, a phone call, or an e-mail once in a while. The intention of this strategy is to build and strengthen your network actively and consistently. You don't have to be a social genius to build strong relationships. Often, just being genuine and letting someone know that you are willing to help or can use some help goes a long way.

Be Helpful and Ask for Help

One of the best strategies on influence and building relationships comes from Robert Cialdini (2001). His research on influence includes the law of reciprocity. Simply put, if you genuinely help someone, they are motivated to help you. Think about it, when you help out someone, it creates a positive bond that has a lasting impact. One way to put this into action is to find ways to leverage your natural strengths and help people who can benefit from your expertise. It doesn't always have to be something that is a major event. It can be as simple as being a sounding board or supporting someone when they need it.

This also works the other way around. You can actually build strong relationships just by asking for some help. High achievers have a tendency to want to figure things out on their own. Although that may be admirable to some, it is not the most effective use of time. If you can use someone's insight or support, it has a lasting impact. Most people naturally want to be helpful. When you enlist someone's help, or help someone, it deepens your relationship with them. This strategy will help you to add to your relationship capital.

Relationship Reaches

When I was in my first year of graduate school, I was told I should read *Fortune* magazine if I wanted to learn more about the business world. The goal was to enhance my business vocabulary and to learn as much as I could about the game of business. By that time, I had learned the value of developing relationships. There was a feature article about a business woman, Cynder Niemela, who was a successful executive coach. There was a picture of her on a yacht with a cell phone as she was coaching an executive.

At the time, that was extremely impressive to me. I found out her contact information and reached out to her. All I did was let her know that I'd appreciate the opportunity to talk with her and learn about what she does. It ended up being a great move. We developed a relationship and she helped me get ready to prepare for a career in consulting. We even presented together at national conferences.

The reason I mention this story is that I believe people want to be helpful and enjoy mentoring others. Of course, there are plenty of people who don't want to give you the time of day. However, it only takes one or two people to truly make an impact in your life. The point is, stretch yourself and reach out to people who are "relationship reachers." People who you don't know, but do what you would love to do or you admire. What's the more important point? Become someone who people want to learn from and get to know, and be someone who is genuine and willing to help others help themselves. Rather than me telling you about the rewards, go for it, and then you'll know.

19

Firefighting and Emotion Commotion

Emotional Intelligence in Action (EIA)

We live and work in a reactive world. It seems to me that more and more companies give out badges of honor to those who take action first and fast. What's wrong with that? It creates a culture of firefighting, where people expect the "first answer" rather than the right answer. I'm all about moving forward fast, but not every time and not at the expense of strategy.

We are constantly reacting to headlines. Our reactive culture has even infiltrated the stock market. If you pay attention to headlines, you'll see how in recent years they have been driving the markets. Oil spills, a crash, a callback, missing quarterly numbers—all of these headlines have driven stock prices down. In my view, the market has overreacted and then corrected. People have one data point, then overreact to the news and make quick decisions. That's usually when I buy, when there is an overreaction. It's an opportunity to stay cool and try to capitalize. I am in no way qualified to give investment or trading advice, but I am qualified to give emotional investment advice.

I've been fortunate to be involved in researching and applying emotional intelligence (EI) for just under two decades. EI in general is a person's ability to be aware of and manage their emotions. What became evident to me is that EI can be learned, and if you apply what you learn, you can make a huge positive impact on yourself and others. It started for me early on; I knew that there was something more to being successful rather than just with traditional intelligence.

When I was studying the psychology of sport and performance at Springfield College's Athletic Counseling program, I began to research EI. At the time, it had not taken off in corporate America yet. I decided to focus my thesis on this concept, but had limited empirical feedback about how to bridge the gap from research to practice. One summer, I was at the American Psychological Association's conference in San Francisco and was walking on a random street. I happened to walk past a person and recognized his face. It was Dr. Peter Salovey, the person who coined the term "emotional intelligence" (Mayer and Salovey, 1997).

Once I realized who it was, I turned around and asked him for a moment of his time. He gave me a lot more than that. He invited me to visit him at his office at Yale. He took the time not only to point my research in the right direction, but also to help me network with others in similar initiatives. Dr. Salovey is now the president of Yale University. His research had a large impact on my work, and his wisdom and grace has had an even larger impact on me.

The business case for EI is clear and has been well researched. The basic case is that people who have high levels of EI are able to be more strategic about how they approach people and business. EI has been found to be a predictor of success in leaders and athletes. If you are interested in more specifics about the business case for EI, the EI Consortium is a solid starting place (*www .eiconsortium.org*).

There are several theories of EI out there, many of them robust. My view is that EI does not have to be complicated; it has to be commonly stated. I created a framework for my clients that bridges theory to practice. I wanted to create something that is business focused and puts a premium on practicality. The question I had was, what do people need in relation to EI to be successful? My answer is *Emotional Intelligence in Action*.

Simple Success Strategy: Emotional Intelligence in Action

Emotional Intelligence in Action (EIA) is *the ability to leverage insight so you can intentionally influence*. The focus is on taking intentional action toward what you want. EIA includes the integration of thinking, feeling, and acting so you can be strategic and get results. It is about taking your EI and putting it into practice. It is a combination of wisdom and action. It is developed through time with new experiences. Wisdom is about making smart choices and responding rather than reacting. Reactions are based on *feelings* and seem automatic, whereas responses are strategic and based on *facts*.

To take it a step further, feelings are the currency that run the world. However warm, fuzzy, or hokey that sounds, it has been played out time and time again in the work I do and the interactions I see around the world. When I have speaking engagements or I advise people on the power of emotion in the workplace, I welcome them to challenge me. And trust me—clients on Wall Street, and top tier talent, challenge me on this point.

Here is my case. No matter what is at the surface, emotion is underneath it. I often ask people why they do what they do. The usual response is for money. My response is: what does money do for you? It buys you things, whether they are needed or not. What do these things do for you? They make you feel safe, important, or secure. Next I ask: what does religion do for you? They will say it gives you a place to go and a purpose, and my response is, yes it does, it gives you a feeling of community, connection, and meaning. Next I ask, what about power, success, or helping others? By this time, most people get it and understand. Although there are multiple reasons for doing things, emotion is somewhere, whether people are aware of it or not. You are free to agree or disagree. All I ask is that you are open to learning how you can use emotion or it will use you.

In order to be successful through time, you need to focus on feelings and facts. Both have value and if you leave out one, the other will have a negative impact. People tend to overemphasize one or the other, especially in times when they are under pressure. In the moment, feelings can seem like facts and guide you in a direction you don't want to go. Feelings are what we associate with facts. For example, if someone says something that upsets you, the fact is that they said something. Your feeling is the impact it had on you.

The important thing to remember is that no matter what the situation and no matter what happens, all feelings come and all feelings go. At times they may seem intense and as if they are going to knock you over, but they will always pass. We give power to feelings. Feelings are not negative or positive; they are neutral and just how we label our experiences. I like to think of it as the weather. Weather will always shift, and the more prepared you are and know what type of weather is coming, the less of an impact it has on you. If it's going to rain, you can bring an umbrella and dress accordingly. I'm not saying that rain doesn't have the potential to bring people down, but we decide how long we stay down and if we want to shift our response to the weather.

Have you ever "lost it" in a conversation? We all have. It's called an emotional hijack, when there is a wave of emotion and it seems like you aren't able to choose what you do next. An example of this may be when someone "gets under your skin" and you have an emotional outburst, also known as losing your composure. This is a common occurrence. With time it can lead to people not viewing you as someone who is credible or in control. The good news is that with some insights and influence you can maintain your composure and be strategic about the decisions you make.

They key is to know your emotional triggers. Emotional triggers are the events, people, sayings, and situations that grab your emotional attention. We all have them and if we aren't aware of them, they have a big impact on how we react in the moment. An example of an emotional trigger is that person in meetings who keeps going off topic and makes the meeting run longer. One of my emotional triggers is injustice or manipulation. If someone is in a powerful position and they bully or treat others with less power poorly, then that is a trigger for me. However, I know that I can protect myself by preparing for those situations and having strategies to deal with them.

The first step is to know your trigger; the second step is to respect it rather than avoid it; and third is to do something to help yourself take the power away from the emotion associated with the trigger. An example would be to remove yourself from the situation or to have something you can say to yourself to maintain your composure. For example, "This is just a temporary feeling and it will pass, and then I can decide what I want to do."

Emotional Intelligence in Action Framework

The EIA framework places emphasis on achieving the desired outcome of your *intentional impact*. The three core elements of the framework are *insight*, *influence*, and *impact*. *Insight* and *influence* are the tools you use to help you reach the *impact* that you want (intentional impact). The three areas within insight and influence are self, social, and situational. The following are descriptions of the core elements outlined in detail.

The EIA framework is a cycle and is an ongoing process you can leverage until you are consistently achieving your *intentional impact*. At first, the *initial impact* you achieve may not be what you want or intend. Even worse, it may be the opposite of what you want. The purpose of having emotional wisdom is to help you be more effective at being aware and taking strategic action.

Let's work through an example of how this framework works in real life. The example I'll use is an executive coaching engagement with a doctor who was the chief, overseeing a critical area of a hospital. Let's call him Doc. When I started working with him, I asked him what was most important to him and what he wanted to accomplish. He said that he wanted to be respected, credible, and build a high-performing team. That was his *intention*: respect, credibility, and his team's high performance. I also asked him what he was doing to achieve what he wanted and how close he was. He responded by saying

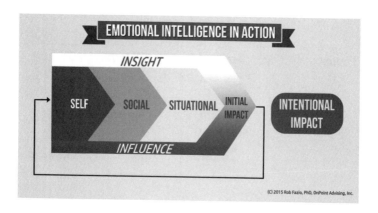

EMOTIONAL INTELLIGENCE IN ACTION

INSIGHT

SELF   SOCIAL   SITUATIONAL   INITIAL IMPACT   INTENTIONAL IMPACT

INFLUENCE

(C) 2015 Rob Fazio, PhD, OnPoint Advising, Inc.

Overview of Emotional Intelligence in Action

Core Element	Domain	The ability to
Insight	Self-Insight	Have awareness of your emotions, thoughts, and how they influence your actions.
	Social Insight	Read verbal and nonverbal cues, emotion in others, and your impact on others.
	Situational Insight	Recognize the power and politics in systems and the business context.
Influence	Self-Influence	Redirect and motivate yourself.
	Social Influence	Engage in effective interpersonal interactions.
	Situational Influence	Initiate positive change to the current setting, culture, business, or industry.
Impact	Initial Impact	The outcome you get that may or may not match your intention.
	Intentional Impact	Your desired outcome that is aligned with your intention.

that he was close except that the team was not following his direct instruction. My goal here was to see what level of *insight* and *influence* he had.

To begin the process, I collected some anonymous feedback from his staff, superiors, and his peers. The messages in the feedback were clear. He was a leader who was feared rather than respected and there was a lot of fighting among his team. This is an example of a disconnect between his *initial impact* and his *intentional impact*. Once I built up some credibility and trust with Doc, I was able to get him to start with thinking about himself. I explained to him that there was a large gap between what he wanted and what he was getting, and it started with him.

Doc had very little self-insight, as he didn't realize how his feelings of insecurity caused him to be overly directive. The short version of this is Doc worked on his ability to be aware when he was under pressure (self-insight) and catch himself in the moment and adapt his communication approach based on the situation and person (self-influence). The result was people started to respect him more, fear him less, and work more effectively together. In other words, through gaining awareness into how his feelings and thoughts were driving his behavior, he became more effective at being strategic and adapting his approach to leadership.

Emotional Hijack Practice

Let's practice learning a little more about an emotional hijack. Picture yourself as someone who just got told that you needed to restructure your organization and let two people go. To make matters worse, this is the second time this year that this has happened, and you were told that there would be no more layoffs. You also assured your team there would be no more layoffs. Put yourself in this situation and experience the situation attaching emotions and thoughts that you might have.

→ What would your initial reaction be?

→ Rate your approximate intensity of emotion(s) you feel. Use a 1 (low) to 10 (high) to identify your emotional intensity.

→ What caused your level of emotional reaction to the degree that you have indicated?

→ What are some of the advantages and disadvantages of reacting this way?

→ How might this affect your communication style in the moment and with your team?

→ What impact might this have on your team's performance? On your credibility?

→ How can you most effectively lead yourself, your team, and your organization through this situation?

It may be the case that you are able to remain remarkably composed and see the positive in this scenario. For many people it is very difficult to not react and be less strategic with themselves and others when a situation has a high intensity of emotion. With time and experience, you will become better at realizing when you are about to experience an emotional hijack. You'll also get better at pulling yourself out of the emotional hijack. This series of questions can help you in all situations to be more strategic in how you manage your potential emotional highjacks.

Emotion is here to stay. You may as well start to obtain insight into yourself, other people, and situations that can help you be more effective at influencing. Getting blind-sided by emotion causes unintended consequences. You won't get it right every time, but I can guarantee you that if you think before you act and act on what you think, you will be more successful at leading yourself and others.

20

Conversation Hesitation

Conversation Confidence

What's our greatest tool to move toward success? It's not money. It's not IQ. It's not even time. It's actually pretty simple and, in fact, I'm leveraging the tool right now. Our greatest tool as we move toward success is conversation. Think about it. How much of your day do you spend in conversations? When we're not in a conversation, we're often consumed with thinking about the last conversation we had or dreading the next conversation we're about to have. As I am sure you have heard dozens of times, it's not what you know, it's who you know. Actually, it's *what you know about who you know* that makes the difference.

Conversations and understanding people are a huge part of our home and work lives. We know that people who are more effective at conversations are simply more successful. The more confident you are in your conversation skills, and the fewer conversations you avoid, the more you are engaged to move toward your goals.

Simple Strategy: Conversation Confidence

The formula for conversation success is to know the foundation for conversations, know the common conversation traps, know your primary conversation style, and know how to read the conversation styles of others. These four foundational conversation keys will allow you to be more confident and become more conversation savvy.

Too often people get caught up with emphasis on the "Golden Rule," which is to treat people as you want to be treated. When it comes to communication, the Golden Rule is actually poor advice. In order to be effective, you want to communicate with people the way *they* want to be communicated with. A simple illustration of this is if you are someone who is extremely direct and results-oriented and you stay direct with someone who prefers a more relational approach. In this case, your messages won't be received. People will be turned off and shut down.

Effective conversations have a natural flow and cadence. When the flow is broken and it goes from a conversation to an awkward interaction, clarity is lost and the conversation becomes a barrier to success and a missed opportunity. Often when a conversation goes wrong, it's because we are speaking a different language and not aligning our conversation style with the person we are communicating. There are several different approaches to conversations. Let's focus on four primary conversation styles so we can identify and leverage preferences. Think of your conversation style as being "righty" or "lefty." It's not that you can't use your other hand, it's just that one feels more natural. The goal is to be able to identify which style to use when and to be versatile. Let's walk through the four conversation preferences and then the four conversation styles.

Conversation Preferences: Reading, Leading, People, and Performance

Reading is about awareness and understanding. The primary concerns are information and learning. People who are reading-oriented tend to ask questions and be inquisitive. *Leading* is about influence, action, and moving toward something. *People* is about relationships and connections. This preference is focused on connection, harmony, teamwork, and collaboration. People who are people-focused tend to be more relational and communicate with emotion. *Performance* is about results and task completion. This preference is focused on getting things completed and as fast as possible. People who are performance-oriented tend to be direct and achievement-oriented.

The Four Conversation Characters

Our preferences in conversations are the best predictors of how we tend to communicate to others. These preferences make up a certain pattern or approach related to communication. I like to call these our conversation characters. I will go over them in detail a bit later in this chapter. For now, let me provide an example. If you are someone who values information and data, you will most likely present information and data when you communicate with others. Though this may feel comfortable to you and bring you success in many conversations, the key is versatility and being able to adapt your conversation style to best communicate with others. There is no "correct" conversation character; they all have strengths and challenges. It's just like learning any other skill. If you choose to, you can become more effective.

In Chapter 15 you will recall we discussed motivational currency. Although there is not a direct correlation, there are core aspects of each conversation style that are aligned with your motivational currency. For example, one of the conversation characters is called an "opener." An opener often has a strong preference toward interacting with people, which means they appreciate relationships and getting along with others. It may be helpful as you read through each of the conversation styles to identify what their motivational currency is.

Based on conversation preferences, there are four possible conversation characters or styles: *the opener, the closer, the calculator,* and *the persuader.* Each of the conversation styles has value and can be effective. The value is in knowing which style you tend to leverage, knowing how to read the conversation style of others, and knowing how to adapt your style. The way to think about this is: Where is the person's focus in a conversation? What comes most

Conversation Characters

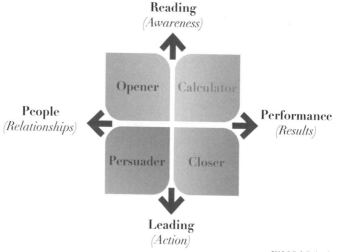

2015 © Rob Fazio, PhD
OnPoint Advising, Inc

naturally to this person in a conversation? Keep in mind there are no correct or incorrect conversation styles, just ones that are more effective in certain situations.

The Opener. The opener conversation style is a combination of reading (awareness) and people (relationships). Those who prefer this style value being cordial and getting along with others in conversations. They focus on understanding and the feelings of others. They focus on gathering information and naturally anticipate their impact on others. In conversations, the opener often asks a lot of questions and is happy to listen in order to learn.

The Closer. The closer conversation style is a combination of a preference for performance (results) and leading (action). A person with this style values getting things done and getting them done fast. He or she tends

Conversation Styles

Conversation Style	Preferences	Marquee Value	Potential Motivational Currency (Someone can have more than one strong motivator)	Potential Challenges
Opener	• Reading 　– Awareness and understanding • People 　– Relationships	Relationship builder Collaborator	• People • Purpose	• Can be perceived as too "nice and passive." • Focuses too much on getting along and making people feel good.
Closer	• Performance 　– Results • Leading 　– Taking action and asserting	Results-driven Speed Direct	• Performance • Power	• Can be perceived as too forceful or uncaring. • Tendency for results over relationships.

Calculator	• Reading
	  – Awareness
	    and
	    understanding
	• Performance
	  – Results
		Accuracy
		Patient
			• Performance
			• Purpose
				• Can be perceived as a "perfectionist" and too detail-oriented.
				• May move too slow and in a structured manner.

Persuader	• People
	  – Relationships
	• Leading
	  – Taking Action
		Influence
		Inspiration
		Moves things
		forward
			• People
			• Power
			• Performance
			• Purpose
				• Can be perceived as out of touch with reality.
				• May not think through the "how" but loves the big-picture story.

to speak directly and in a concise manner. Their emphasis is on outcome.

The Calculator. The calculator conversation style is a combination of a preference for reading (awareness) and performance (results). This person values understanding and getting things right. He or she appreciates logic and accuracy. In conversations, this person can speak slowly and ask a lot of questions.

The Persuader. The persuader conversation style is a combination of people (relationships) and leading (persuading). A person with this style enjoys influencing and making an impact. He or she values telling a story and what makes an impression.

The value is in realizing the diversity in our conversation styles. Just as with what motivates someone, there are things that help you be more effective in conversations. The more you can read before you lead in a conversation, the higher the probability of success you will have.

Section 4

Accelerating

21

Blurry Vision
Vision with Precision

Having a vision is fun; vision with precision gets it done.
—Stephen Covey

Begin with the end in mind. Put your intention out there and it will be yours. We've all heard the catchy statements about vision. It is true; if you don't know where you are going, you will likely end up somewhere you don't want to be. Although imagining yourself being wealthy and successful or on a yacht enjoying a fine drink may make you feel good, it won't get you there. It's not the vision alone that leads to success. It's the vision plus insight into how to reach the vision. I actually think that people who are "visionaholics" get in the way of their own success because they don't focus on what to do and how to do it. The result is they just wait for things to happen for them.

I can remember early on in my doctoral studies, a friend of mine and I were facing a time when our funding was going to be in jeopardy for our work. As we were walking down the road, my friend said that he was going to go home and pray and I said that I was going home to map out what I need, what I want, and who can help me make it happen. Then I started contacting people. Both of us were in the same situation, yet we took two completely different approaches. I appreciate seeing where I need to go, how to get there, and having laser focus until I'm there, or I change where I want to go.

It's not just my point of view; there is also research to support the idea that a vision focused on the end state without the starting point and steps gets you nowhere fast. Psychologists Lien Pham and Shelley Tailor from the University of California (Pham and Taylor, 1999) put students into two groups. They asked one group of students (Group A) to visualize how great it would be to get a high grade. The other group of students (Group B) *wasn't* asked to visualize the positive feelings associated with the end state of a high grade. Both groups of students were asked to keep track of the actual hours they spent studying. In other words, how much work they put into reaching a goal. Even though the group that visualized the positive feelings associated with a good grade only did this for a few minutes, it had a significant impact on the amount of time they studied as well as their grades. The group of students (Group A) that visualized the positive feelings ended up studying less and ended up with lower grades. The visualization may have made them feel good, but it did not prepare them for success and therefore set them up for the failure. My view on this situation is that the students from Group A, who associated the positive feelings with the outcome, became overconfident and were not aware and/or not realistic about how to get what they wanted.

What makes the point even more clearly is that the researchers had a third group of students (Group C). This group was asked to visualize the "how" or process of getting an A for a few moments a day. This means they were asked to get into more detail and visualize how and what they would do to get an A. Compared to Group A that just visualized the outcome of getting an A, and to Group B that wasn't asked to do anything, Group C that was asked to visualize the "how" ended up studying more hours and earned higher exam grades than both other groups. The researchers concluded that visualizing the steps to prepare them for success put them in a more realistic and practical vision to succeed.

I have seen the same story play out again and again. Countless executives I work with tell stories of motivational speakers who get them fired up by seeing success. Seeing success is not enough; you also have to see the steps. The better you are at seeing the steps, the more prepared you will be for not tripping over the missteps. It may feel great and be a lot of fun to visualize success, but that's not what's going to get you there. What will get you there is vision with precision.

Simple Success Strategy: Vision with Precision

Intention without follow-through is like a golf swing with no ball to hit. We all do it. We get caught up in what could be and what we want. The most straightforward, simple success strategy includes three essential steps: vision, envision, and revision. *Vision* is where you want to go. *Envision* is where you are, what you are getting, and how you get to where you want to go. Finally, *revision* is what you need to change to get to where you want to be. In the revision stage, you can either change your vision or change your envision (steps). That is the most direct approach. However, let's add a little more depth so you have some more support as you create visions. The more in-depth process will give you another tool to reach a wider range of people and will be more helpful in more complex situations or changes for when you are leading others.

Setting a Vision for Yourself: Aspiration, Concentration, and Motivation

I'm a big believer in the philosophy that people are naturally drawn to and want to follow people who have credibility and a plan to move forward. A core aspect of success is being able to create and communicate a vision that people are inspired to work toward. Vision without a plan to execute is just a wish list. It's time to change the aspiration to concentration, which will create more motivation.

Aspiration. Aspiration is what you want. It is what you are moving toward and want to achieve. An aspiration can be challenging and, at the same time, it needs to be realistic and obtainable. This doesn't mean that it has to be something that will take you years to achieve; it just means that it is different than just a dream. It is something that you can achieve and are ready and willing to achieve. You can have different aspirations for career and life, or an aspiration that combines them both. An aspiration involves knowing where you are and identifying what you need to do to travel to somewhere else. Consistent with everything in this book, the keys are raising awareness, taking action, and keeping things simple as you move toward success.

Aspiration example: I want to be known as a strong strategic thinker and get a senior level role that involves strategy.

Concentration. Concentration isn't easy, but it can be simple. This is where you outline the "how," the process, the steps. It includes laser focus on what you need to do to reach your aspiration. If you get the concentration piece right, people should be able to see your process and progress.

Concentration example: I am going to focus on building my understanding of what it takes to become a thoughtful leader and effective strategic thinker. The first step I will take is to make a list of people inside and outside my organization who are strong strategic thinkers. I will do informational interviews of anyone who has credibility and is known as a strategic thinker. I'll make a list of questions that will help me learn more about strategic thinking. I will also identify three Websites where people talk about strategy. I will write a page about my approach to strategic thinking and add to it as I learn more. Once I have a point of view on strategy, I'll talk to my boss and let them know about an initiative that I can take on that involves strategic thinking.

Motivation. Motivation is the fuel that gets you through your concentration and to your aspiration. This is all about keeping yourself engaged, having grit, and staying mentally fit. In order to stay laser focused on the concentration phase, you need to find ways to stay on task. This can be done by rewarding yourself with things that you enjoy, or it can be done by reminding yourself how much it would mean to you to achieve your aspiration. In Chapter 15, I outlined the concept of *motivational currency*. Knowing your motivational currency will give you a more direct path and keep you engaged, as there will be many ups and downs in your journey.

Motivation example: I am going to make a list of rewards aligned with my motivational currency (that is, performance, people, power, and purpose). I will keep myself motivated by rewarding myself with doing something I enjoy after I complete three informational interviews.

Setting a Vision for Others: See, Feel, Think, Act

Intention is powerful for a moment. Intention with impact is powerful for a lifetime. Recall what I mentioned previously. We judge ourselves on our intentions and we judge others by their impact. It's a natural and normal tendency, but one we want to manage. Creating a vision with precision is simply a way to organize your line of sight in the right direction and give you something to work toward, as well as help you outline the steps. The more proficient you become at identifying and creating a vision, the more likely people will be to follow you.

Seeing isn't believing; achieving is believing. People want to follow people who are able to provide them with hope and a plan. When you are in a leadership position you can create positive momentum by creating and communicating a vision with precision. It feels great for you and others to communicate a vision. However, if you don't let people (and yourself, for that matter) know how to reach the vision, you will get labeled as someone who is unrealistic or, worse, "salesy." The art of an effective vision is to give people something to work toward and get them started.

An effective vision has four essential accelerating elements: *see*, *feel*, *think*, and *act*. These elements work with you to move toward something you want so you don't get stuck in what you don't want. Vision with precision is a recipe for getting things done quickly and accurately. Vision with precision brings out passion that is lasting. The key is to provide enough information in a variety of ways that taps into people's motivational currency. This can be done by tapping into as many senses as possible. This means connecting with people in multiple ways so you provide them with an emotional hook in a positive way. The goal is to create initiative. After all, there isn't something much better at work than having people do what is important without having to tell them what to do. A clear vision with the following components not only brings you closer to where you want to go, but it gets people motivated to work with you rather than against you. Another simple way to remember what you need in a vision is to just think of it as using your eyes, heart, head, and hands.

See (eyes). *Where* are we going? People want to have something to move toward together. A line of sight into where you are going gives people guidance and helps them move forward. When you help people "see," you are answering one main question: where are we going? This includes as much information as you can give for what the destination looks like. Think of this as painting a picture for people. Think of this as communicating an image to people, just like the one on the cover of a puzzle. When you let people know what the big picture is, you can build on to this direction.

Feel (heart). *Why* are we going there? In my view, nothing is more powerful than emotion. Purpose taps into emotion. The main questions you are answering when you create the "feel" is why are we doing this and what is the purpose? People get behind a purpose. The purpose doesn't have to be sophisticated or over engineered communication. It can be as simple as clearly telling people what the value is in achieving the vision. One approach is to use an "if, then" statement. If we do X, then we will be better positioned to achieve Y. It's also very valuable to let people know what's in it for them and how it will impact them.

Think (head). *How* will I get there and *who* is responsible? Think is all about the plan. It's the how and who aspect of the strategy. This is where some of the details of a plan get communicated. In this step in the vision process you let people know who will be playing what part. It's essentially the roadmap to the vision. The more specific you can be, the better. Set up milestones and metrics. Include how you will measure progress, success, and failure. However, it's more important to be transparent and allow for changes or shifts in the plan so people know they need to be adaptive and versatile.

Act (hands). *What* is the first step and action item? Action! This is where you communicate what the action steps will be and what the first step is and when. This is different than the "think" aspect of the vision in that it is more detailed and specific. The focus is on doing rather than just planning.

A vision can be a moving target and a working progress. In the "think" phase, ensure you have a milestone when you will evaluate progress. The way you can evaluate your progress is through paying attention to insight, hindsight, and foresight. Insight is what you are learning during the process and what enhancements or innovation you may want to add. Hindsight is about evaluating progress, seeing what is going well, and what needs to change. Foresight is looking forward and anticipating what is to come that will enable or potentially disable the progress.

I have learned a lot through the years about "vision." What has had the biggest impact is knowing that focusing forward counts a lot and what counts more is how to get there and taking action. I remember hearing about a 2007 McKinsey and Company study (Dye and Sibony, 2007) that highlighted three quarters of executive participants in strategic planning. Half of them were not happy with the process and less than a quarter used the strategic plan. You have the opportunity to see, feel, think, and act. Take advantage of it and you will not only excel, but you will also inspire others to do the same.

22

The Complexity of Change

Focus on Facts, Feelings, and the Future

Change. The word is one of the worst and most over-used. Yet, it also has the potential to create the best in people at the worst of times. When will change happen? The answer is early and often. It's not a matter of "if," it's a matter of "when." I am always surprised when people are surprised about how much change is part of their lives. It's the only thing we know will happen in life and business. Change is essential for growth. Granted, not all change is good, but all change is an opportunity to create something good. It's an opportunity to demonstrate your ability to be resilient and versatile.

Change is tough because it happens at different levels of the organization at different times and at different speeds. Let's use a company I work with as example of how change can be a disruptor of productivity. This company, let's call them Simple Co., decides at the board level that they want to change how the company is perceived in the market and they want to enhance their brand. The higher ups made a decision that the company would be better served and gain more market share with a higher-end brand. Therefore, Simple Co.'s board decided it would market itself as a value-add service provider rather than a product company. This means they will focus more on quality service, long-term relationships, and meeting needs, rather than just selling what they have to sell.

The first thing to happen is the top people in the organization look at the pros and cons of the board's decisions. There is a good amount of resistance and some people are dead against the move and think they will lose customers. They look at it from all angles and, with time, people realize the benefits outweigh the costs. They make the decision to go along with the board. They come to the conclusion that this change in brand will result in a long-term return on investment. After that decision is made, the business case is clear as day to the CEO, CFO, and head of sales at the corporate level. That sounds great doesn't it?

The next step would be simply to just inform each Vice President of Sales and roll out the new brand-enhancing initiative, right? Not even close. What corporate fails to realize is the process they went through. They don't recall that there was actually a time where they themselves had concerns, opposition, and resistance. Every level of the business is in a different place when it comes to what the change thought leaders call "the change curve." Having resistance to change is normal and what's critical to keep in mind is that when change hits, it hits each person in different ways. It's all about how you take the hit.

For leaders, the key is to be patient and persistent. You need to realize where people are on the change curve and meet them where they are with a genuine concern for helping them navigate their resistance to change. In this instance, the high-level executives were able to move pretty quickly once they had a line of sight into the financials and the market share they would gain. In other words, they saw the clear business case, partly because they had a line of sight into all the factors. The lower people are in the organization, the less information they have and the more they look for it.

The goal is to accelerate people's distance between resistance and acceptance. You want people to move forward as quickly as possible. Once the case for change is clear and the vision for the future is more powerful than acceptance of the current situation, you get progress. A simple way to look at this is that *hope and a plan are greater than pushback.* I use the term "hope" to demonstrate that it is important to tap into emotion in some way, shape, or form. Believe me, I am a "get it done" type of person. However, I know the value of connecting with people, and the best way to do this is by combining the elements of hope and action. Pushback can come in all forms. It can be complaining, it can be resistance to doing something different, or it can be just getting stuck. It happens to us all. When you build a case for change that includes hope and a plan, it motivates people to take action toward the future rather than getting stuck in the past.

Simple Success Strategy: Focus on Facts, Feelings, and the Future

The case is built, change will happen and happen often. It's not the change that makes the difference; it's the response to change that makes the difference. There are several change management frameworks out there. I've leveraged many of them in my consulting work. What I realized is that there are three simple success factors linking the best approaches that I've seen work. The success factors are: facts, feelings, and future. Where people go wrong is they focus too much on one and not the others. It's a natural instinct to go with what we know, especially in times of stress. Versatility and velocity are the keys to effective change management and dealing with transitions. The integration of the three is what brings about success in situations of change. In my experience, when merger and change initiatives fail it's because of a lack of due diligence. What does this mean? The "business" people don't pay attention to the "busy" people. This means the executives are disconnected from the cultural implications of change. If it's two companies merging, the human and cultural element is overlooked by the thrill of the business deal.

Before I outline each of the success factors, I want to offer a caveat. I know that change is not easy, and I know that there will always be a tendency to procrastinate and get stuck. What I am suggesting is that you take attempts at positive action. By focusing on facts, feelings, and the future, you will have a higher probability of success.

Facts

Facts and logic—they are what they are. It doesn't get simpler than what the facts are. Facts are the logical, technical, and business side of things. In situations of change, knowing what is happening, why it's happening, and how it impacts the people and the business is critical. When you focus on facts, you temporarily keep emotion out of the equation. You just look at things as they are and how logically they need to be. The core question to ask yourself and others is, "What are the facts?"

Feelings

Feelings, just like facts, are a data point. You just don't want feelings to be your only data point. A focus on feelings allows you to anticipate how the change is impacting you and others emotionally. There is nothing more powerful than being aware of the emotions you are experiencing and being in tune with the emotions of others. Acknowledging and validating people's experience goes a long way. Emotions drive behavior. The more you are in tune with your emotions and those of others, the more loyalty you build and the quicker you can get through change. The core question to ask yourself and others is, "How are people going to react and how will they feel?"

Future

There is nothing more challenging and scary for people during change than a murky future. As stated earlier, people want hope and a plan so they can work toward something tangible. By being future-oriented, the goal is to create positive momentum. Small wins yield big results. The core question to ask yourself and others is, "What are we moving toward and how can I help us to get there?"

Having a framework in which you can communicate the facts, being aware of and acting on feelings, and focusing on the future allows you to tap into different aspects of what is important to people. I find that, too often, people are in a reactive mindset in dealing with the repercussions of change. William Bridges, who is a prominent thought leader related to dealing with transitions, explained that change is external and transition is internal (2009). I found his wisdom to be powerful. It's the difference between having something happen to you and something happening within you.

23

Losing Focus and Lack of Follow-Through

Practical Prioritization

For the next 30 seconds I want you to have laser focus on what you are about to read. Ready, go. Focus is what gets you from where you are to where you want to be. Everyone has too much to do with too little time and too little resources. Focus is the remedy for excuses. When you focus, you move forward. We all have the ability to focus. It's time to find your focus.

Okay, you can take it easy now. When I asked you to have laser focus for the next 30 seconds, what did you do? What did you say to yourself? How did you focus? The answer to these questions is the key to your focus and priority. Dr. Ken Ravizza, sport psychology consultant to professional athletes, taught this simple success strategy to me. He is one of the best in the world. He applies this approach when teaching athletes about focus.

The key is in getting in touch with what it means to focus for you. For some, it's taking a deep breath and saying something positive to themselves. For others, it's clearing their mind or sitting upright and making themselves feel focused. For me, it's about getting in my own zone. What I mean by this is I know what to say to myself and what to do to get in my own zone. It is different for everyone. By answering the earlier questions, it will give you a good sense of what it means for you to get in your own zone.

The biggest mistake people make with setting priorities is they confuse them with preferences. A preference is something that is nice to have or nice to complete. A priority is something that comes first, as in prior to your preference. That's why "prior" is the root of the word. We are all bombarded by priorities on top of priorities. Too many priorities actually have the opposite effect and when you prioritize too many things, you are just doing stuff.

My first job out of college was at the flagship Tiffany and Company store on 5th Avenue in New York City. I got the job through a special friend, Pete Theodorakos, who was in charge of taking in repairs. My job was in customer service. Although this may seem like a simple and straightforward job, it was anything but simple. Our role was to talk with customers and help them resolve any issues with jewelry. The challenge was that every customer's request was his or her personal immediate priority. I learned so much from Pete and the jewelers who fixed these high-end items. Above the jewelers' workspace was a sign that said, "Should I rush, the rush job, I was rushing when you rushed in?" It was a great reminder that in customer's minds, everything was a priority and we had to find a way to prioritize what was actually a priority.

The interesting thing was the nights in the same year I worked in a psychiatric treatment facility. There, prioritization was clear. I was a mental health worker and they used a triage system. Priorities were very clear at this job. If a code was called, it meant someone was in danger of hurting themselves or someone else. Codes took priority over everything. We didn't have to think. We just knew to respond.

The truth is, in our everyday lives, priorities are not going to be that clear, so we need to create clarity, and the best way to do that is to have a system and common language so we can focus forward. If you are a leader of people, the best thing you can do is have the people who report to you adopt a prioritization strategy and teach it to others. You want to have a clear prioritization framework for yourself as well. The key is to have a way to prioritize that is practical and easy to use.

Simple Success Strategy: Practical Prioritization

You need to do what is true for you. As simple as this may sound, it works. It doesn't mean that you don't want to reach outside your comfort zone. What it does mean is that unless your priority strategy is going to get put into practice consistently, it is useless. I've had the opportunity to learn from people who are the best of the best. I'm certain a common characteristic of their pathway to success is discipline. It's not sexy and doesn't make the headlines, but discipline works. I heard a story about Michael Phelps (I say "heard" because I don't know if this is a fact) that illustrated the importance of developing habits and the cost of missing practice. The main point was that when Phelps misses a day of training, it takes him months to recover. I'm not sure if this is true or not, but what I do know is that once you lose your focus and discipline, it costs a lot. Stay focused, stay disciplined, and get it done now so you don't have to pay for it later.

It comes down to knowing what gives you the best return on your investment of time. A guideline that has proven to lead to success is to focus the large majority of your time and energy on your critical priorities. The Pareto Principle, or 80/20 rule, has been popularized through the years and is aligned with this philosophy. It stems from the work of Vilfredo Pareto (1848–1923), who was an Italian sociologist and economist. Through the years, there have been several interpretations of this principle. However, what holds true is that when you focus your energy and time on your top priorities, it pays off and leads you toward success. Be careful of getting distracted by things that are not aligned with your top priorities. This gives you a way to guide yourself for yourself.

Practical prioritization is about finding a way to focus in a way that is clear and easy. The framework for practical prioritization can be used at work or in your personal life. The goal is to use one strategy that you make a habit and can teach to others so it becomes as simple and automatic as starting your car. Practical prioritization involves three steps: 1) Put your priorities into three categories; 2) Prioritize your priorities; and 3) Decide to do it or not.

The Three Categories

I believe the best way to prioritize is to categorize your priorities into three buckets: personal, professional, and passion. This will help you be laser focused in the three key areas of your life. You can apply practical prioritization to each of these areas. The *personal* bucket is just what it sounds like. This bucket is about your personal life. It can be something around health, your relationships, or something else in your personal life. The *professional* bucket is about work. This includes what you need to get done in order to be successful in your career. A good guide in relation to the professional bucket is to include which priorities are important to your direct boss. The *passion* bucket is about you and what energizes you. This can be a talent that you want to further develop, a hobby you want to dedicate more time to, or it can be just what you love to do.

Prioritize Your Priorities

This step is all about knowing what counts. You will have more priorities than you can actually accomplish. Priorities bombard all of us, but not all of us use a filter to determine what to do first. In order to effectively prioritize your priorities, you need to be clear on what your criteria is.

Decide to Do it or Not: The 1-2-3 of Priority

For each priority, make a list of tasks. The most straightforward way to prioritize tasks is to make it as simple as 1-2-3. The first step is to make a list of all the tasks that you need to complete in relation to a priority at the start of your week. Once you have your list, mark a 1, 2, or 3 next to each task; 1 represents something that has to be done today no matter what; 2 represents something that you aren't sure about; 3 represents something that you can put off until tomorrow. Once you have a number next to each task, go back and change all of your 2s to either a 1 or a 3. This will force you to be crystal clear on what tasks are actually in immediate need of attention.

Calibration Conversation

An additional simple strategy I'd like to offer is the calibration conversation. This simple approach is one for people who need to lead others. It helps everyone win. Clarity is king. Here's how this works. Ask the people who work for you to identify what they think their top three priorities are and what they think your top three priorities are. Then you write down the same. Have a calibration conversation once a month. The conversations bring up gaps you weren't aware of and provides each of you an opportunity to evaluate your expectations.

When it comes to ambition, the truth is that we all have limited time and energy to keep up with work and life demands. The most important success factor in making sure you are getting it right is to have an approach and stick to it. Select an approach that works for you, or create your own.

24

The Stall

Refuel, Repurpose, and Re-energize

I love flying. It's always been a passion of mine. Every noise that stresses passengers out before take-off intrigues me. To me, they are a series of questions. Each sound has a story, and I love trying to figure out what each sound means. I took a few flying lessons (I never completed getting my license for a variety of reasons, and kudos to all of you who were able to reach that goal). As part of the lessons, my instructor would intentionally take me through "stalls" so I could learn what causes them and how to get out of them. The basic principle is, when an airplane stalls it's because of a loss of "lift" and an increase in "drag." Well now, isn't that a pretty solid metaphor for stalls or becoming burnt out at work or life?

We will all have times in our lives where we have "stalls" or periods of time where we aren't passionate or are disengaged. It's a natural part of our lives. It's okay to get stuck; but if you want to be successful, it's not okay to stay stuck. Just like every sound on an airplane tells you something, so does every warning signal in your situational stall. The key is to become good at knowing what makes you stall and how to pull out of it. Take your engagement into your own hands. The best self-engagement strategy is the one that you use. Identify strategies that work for you and use them. Make them a habit and you won't have to think, it will just be a positive habit.

Simple Success Strategy: Refuel, Repurpose, and Re-energize

The actual way to manage a stall in flight is to put your nose down and increase throttle. The idea is to regain airspeed and lift. Putting this into the context of work and life, when you stall or hit a wall, the key is to focus forward fast. The goal is to not only regain control, but to also soar and to get back in your groove.

Refuel

With all the setbacks that are out there, it's important to take time for yourself. Though this may sound simplistic, it works. Our minds, just like our bodies, need a break. In my work with athletes, it was common for them to work their bodies too hard and the coach would then give them a day off, so they can perform later. The same thing goes for our minds. Sometimes the best thing you can do for yourself is to refuel.

The way to refuel is by knowing what relaxes you or brings you joy. For some, this may be spending time with friends, watching a movie, or listening to music. It may be a combination of things. They key is to realize that if you don't give yourself time and space to refuel, you will burn out. Once you burn out, it's very hard to get back on fire and move toward your goals.

Repurpose

There are several ways to *repurpose*. Purpose and passion are strong internal drivers that keep people going. The way to repurpose is by answering a few key questions:

→ Why is it important to me to be successful?
→ What will it feel like when I reach my goal?
→ What would it be like if I failed?
→ What is meaningful about the work I am doing currently?
→ Who else is the work I am doing important to?
→ What needs to change so I am focused on what's important to me?

While you are focusing on repurposing, you may realize that there isn't enough meaning in what you are working on. That's okay and, in fact, it's one of the positives that can come out of going through a stall. Some people spend their entire lives and careers focused on the wrong things, things that have no meaning or purpose to them.

There is nothing more powerful for success than focusing on purpose. It is about ensuring that you are prioritizing and spending the right time on things that matter to you and that pay dividends. When you refocus, you recalibrate and remind yourself of what is important and what you want to accomplish.

A strategy that is helpful in focusing on your purpose is to have a cue word that snaps you into focus. This is something that athletes use to stay focused and to concentrate. The way to use a cue word is to think of a word that gives you confidence. It can be something as simple as "Go" or "Focus." The idea is that when you give yourself something to reconnect you to your purpose, you will move that purpose more efficiently.

Re-Energize

If you don't have fuel in your tank, where you want to drive doesn't matter! Let's face it, work is challenging, life is challenging, and having a work-life balance is even more challenging. It's our own responsibility to intentionally mix in things that we love and love to do and make them a part of our pathway to success. The first step is to know what you enjoy and what you get excited about. I remember a wife of a friend of mine talking about how her husband hated getting up early in the morning and was always late. However, on a day that he was golfing, he got up effortlessly and was always early.

You are not always going to find things that you love at work that you can do all day—well, unless you become a leadership adviser—but you can find some things that you enjoy. Make a list of all the things that you enjoy doing at work and outside of work. Then ensure you are doing these things at least once a week. Hopefully, you can weave in some of these activities once a day. A good strategy is that once you have a master list of re-energizers, you can use that list like a menu. Hold yourself accountable to do something to recharge your battery.

All of us need to know what gets us energized. The more energized we are, the more we can energize others. Think back to a time when you were in a job and you weren't able to participate in any tasks that you enjoyed. For a people-driven individual, it may be that you were only working on completing meaningless tasks. For a performance-oriented person, it may have been you were consistently stuck in conversations for the sake of talking with others. If you consistently deprive yourself of enjoyment, you will eventually burn out, become apathetic or, even worse, become mediocre.

Take Growth STEPS

Once you have your purpose, fuel, and energy, ensure you are stepping in the right direction. Every journey, no matter the distance, begins with one step. Growth STEPS are action steps toward our desired destinations. This concept comes from Hold the Door for Others, a nonprofit organization that specializes in helping people take steps forward despite adversity (Fazio and Fazio, 2006). It can be applied to any goal-setting process, whether it is personal or professional.

Growth STEPS are essential because they provide us with concrete ways we can take control of ourselves and begin to move toward our objectives. Taking Growth STEPS does not mean that there are not barriers or external challenges. It's quite the opposite. I acknowledge potential speed bumps and roadblocks that can impact us (for example, changes in the market, regulations, etc.). However, the focus is on what you can control as opposed to what you can't control.

In order to move toward your desired outcomes, you need to create Growth STEPS that are practical, engaging, easy to follow, and effective. Growth STEPS need to be *Specific, Time-oriented, Emotional, Positive*, and *Self-controlled*. In the following, you will be presented with a description of each characteristic and examples. Executives who take the time to write down their STEPS and ensure they meet the following criteria are much more likely to achieve their desired results.

- **S**—Specific and measurable (has to be clear and able to be measured).
- **T**—Time-oriented (needs to have an element of when).
- **E**—Emotional (connected to what you want and are invested in).
- **P**—Positive (needs to have an element of moving forward).
- **S**—Self-controlled (actions under your control).

Specific. Growth STEPS need to be specific and measurable. Someone who does not know you should be able to know whether or not you have completed your growth step.

Example (not specific): I will *take time* to be strategic *more often.*

Example (specific): On the first Monday of every month, I will have scheduled time to be strategic and think through my approach to talent management and leadership.

Time-oriented. An effective growth step is one that has an element of time. You know when it is completed.

Example: I will talk with three people *a month* and give them feedback on what they are doing well and what I would like to see them do differently.

Emotional. Growth STEPS need to include an emotional connection to you. They need to be something that *you* want to accomplish and something that you are invested in.

Example: *I want* to increase *my* self-awareness by keeping a journal three times a week.

Positive. Growth STEPS need to be stated positively so you know they are helping you grow and move forward.

Example (negative): I *am not* going to be negative and doubt my confidence.

Example (positive): I *am* going to remain positive by saying positive statements to myself and others even when things are not going my way.

Self-controlled. Growth STEPS need to be under your control. They need to be actions that you have control over and where you are the deciding factor of whether they are completed or not.

Example: I am going to ask for feedback on my leadership style once a day in the morning.

Desired Destination (outcome). This is the end result you want to work toward. For example, increasing your financial acumen or emotional intelligence.

If you are intentional and practice your ability to refuel, repurpose, and re-energize, you will be better equipped to deal with lulls in life. The Growth STEPS process will guide you as you make your desired outcomes and goals more concrete.

25

The Pressure Cooker

Control, Capability, and Connection

If you focus on and keep telling people how stressed you are, not only will you be right, but you will stress them out as well.

Stress isn't going anywhere. It will be with you for the rest of your life and it's not necessarily a bad thing. Stress used to be something that literally debilitated me; now, with the right mindset, it's something that motivates me. I'd actually go as far as to say that I enjoy a little pressure and stress. Now trust me, it took me a long time and a lot of work on myself to get there. I was such a worrier that I had stomach pains and my parents brought me to a specialist. I remember drinking a pink shake so they could try to figure out why my stomach was always upset. After a good amount of discussion with a pediatrician, they decided to talk to my kindergarten teacher. What they found was that I was a very anxious little boy. I was so anxious that I would hide under the table in school. Why did I hide under the table? I hid because my teacher would yell at other kids and I was always worried that I would be next. What's my point? I was just a nervous kid and being too nervous can be debilitating.

The pressure and stress we all feel is very real. What is even more real is our ability to counter the stress with some skills and strategies. I can remember working with the CEO of a Fortune 500 company. Many CEOs are high caliber, Ivy League, brilliant people, as he was. When my first and pointed piece of advice to him was to exercise and have stress management strategies, he was not happy. He was so unhappy that he reached out to my boss and let it be known that he did not find his feedback conversation helpful.

It was my job to provide him with feedback from his employees. There were all types of feedback on his command and control style, his business strategy, how he was running the company, etc. Of all the things that people said about him, there was one thing that stood out: pressure. He was not seen as someone who could handle pressure and stress. No one wants to follow someone who can't handle pressure. As pressure goes up, people go back to their default style, and if your default style is command and control, it can create an atmosphere that no one wants to be around.

One day I was watching the news in relation to riots. I heard a woman say, "You can only put so much pressure in a pressure cooker before it blows up." I thought that was a profound statement. Some pressure helps us perform, but too much pressure brings us to a breaking point or at least to a point where our performance and productivity decreases. It's important to keep in mind that not all stress and pressure is bad. It's the chronic day after day stress that gets to us with time and has a negative impact. There is an old story about a frog and a pan of water. The story goes that a frog hopped into a pan of very hot water and immediately jumped out. That's what we would all call acute stress. Another time, the frog was sitting in a pan of cool water on a stove. The water slowly heated up until it was too hot for the frog to survive. That is called chronic stress. When things happen with time and become a norm, we aren't aware of how they impact us. That's why it's so important to be aware of your stress signals and have stress strategies.

Stress is a big part of all of our lives and affects us all in different ways. Three decades ago, stress was not a common expression at all. However, in today's fast-paced business world, the word "stress" is as common as the words Facebook or Gmail. Stress affects all of us on a daily basis in a variety of settings; but what is stress? For our purposes, we'll define stress as anything that is *perceived* as a threat to one's well-being and elicits a physiological and psychological response. The word *perceived* is key and the most important word in this definition. I have come to realize in my life that perception is nine-tenths of the law, and just by being aware of this, my life has changed drastically for the better.

Stress comes from many places. There are three core sources of stress. Most of our stress comes from a perceived lack of control, lack of capability, and lack of connection. As you directly and intentionally build your skill sets in these three areas, it will naturally build your confidence. The higher your confidence, the more effective buffer you have to all types of stress.

Simple Success Strategy: Control, Capability, and Connection

The best way to combat stress is to face the core three sources of stress (lack of control, capability, and connection) head on. There are passive stress management techniques and active stress management techniques. An example of passive stress management would be watching a television show. An active stress management technique would be exercising, doing deep breathing, or visualization.

Active stress management techniques are more effective because you are creating your focus and you are getting your body involved with helping you buffer the impact of stress. In my work with athletes, we spent a lot of time helping people understand their body and mind connection. They work in sync. If you relax your body, it relaxes your mind and vice versa. The opposite is also true; if you stress out your mind, you will stress out your body. There is also a business case for stress. It is very difficult to be strategic and think of the big picture if you are stressed.

Control

When people perceive they don't have control over a situation, or even other people, it can be stressful. The most interesting aspect of this cause of stress is that, in reality, we have control over very little. One of the only things we do have control over is how we respond to situations and people. The most effective strategy related to control is very simple. Take a piece of paper and fold it in half lengthwise. On the left side at the top, write "Can't Control" and on the right side at the top, write "Can Control." When times are tough and there is stress, this simple strategy will help you categorize what you can control and what is out of your control. The intention is to spend your time and focus on the things that you can control.

Capability

When a task or role exceeds your perceived ability to succeed, it causes stress. As pressure goes up, so does your performance, but if there is so much pressure that it rattles your confidence to deliver, it creates more stress. The key is to continue to build your capability and skills. Let's focus on one skill related to managing stress. Then you can continue to build your capability by adding new skills you learn.

One skill is visualization. Right now we are talking about visualization as a tool to reduce stress and relax. This is different than when I was walking you through how to use vision in relation to success in Chapter 21. In Chapter 21, the focus was related to driving action, and now it is about creating relaxation. Visualization isn't for everyone. Actually, when I was being trained in imagery and visualization for my work with athletes, I was a skeptic. Now I'm all in and I practice and teach it all the time.

When you visualize, you connect your mind and body to a desired performance. Effective visualization starts with a foundation of deep breathing to clear your mind and relax yourself. There are several effective deep-breathing strategies that are easily accessible via iTunes or just a Google search away. It's important to take breathing exercises slowly and breathe deeply from your diaphragm and stomach area rather than short sharp breaths from your chest. If you become light-headed at any time, stop the breathing exercise.

The way I practice deep breathing is to take a deep inhale as I slowly count to eight. Then I exhale to a count of eight or until I have completely exhaled. I repeat that slowly a few times while saying to myself, I am confident, I am comfortable, I am capable. Then, once I feel relaxed and I'm in a pattern of effective breathing, I incorporate some visualization. I choose to visualize myself on a boat looking out at the horizon. When you visualize, you want to try and include as many of your senses as possible. In my example, I include what the breeze feels like on my arms, what the heat of the sun feels like on my skin, what the smell of salt water smells like, what I see in the distance, and what I am feeling and thinking. The more specific and detailed you can be, the more effective it is. Just keep breathing deeply and saying relaxing things to yourself.

It is good to practice this a few times a week for 20 minutes at a time. It's just like any other skill; the more you practice it, the better you will be at it, and the more rewards you will reap. In order to prepare for this, make a list of your "happy place" and describe it in detail. Again, visualization isn't for everyone, but I have seen it decrease people's level of stress and increase people's ability to perform under pressure.

Connection

In research that I conducted with the nonprofit Hold the Door for Others (Fazio and Fazio, 2006), we found that the most critical factor in helping people navigate stressful or adverse situations was other people. Social support is a tremendous resource, especially in times of stress. The more meaningful connections you can build, the more opportunities you will have to talk through your stressors and get support. Sometimes, just by talking through what pressure you are under helps you figure it out. Sometimes, it's just a matter of knowing that you have some people on your team to support you.

Your Stress Strategy

It's important to be intentional and have a plan. Expect stress to be part of your life and it will have less power over you. The following are some guiding questions and statements to help you take an active approach to managing stress:

→ Describe a stressful situation that you would like to work on.
→ How has this stressor affected you thus far?
→ What have you done thus far to deal with this stressor?
→ List three stress strategies that you can use for this stressor.

→   Pick one that you will use for a week.

→   Who can support and challenge you to ensure you are applying this technique and sticking with it?

→   Write three reasons why you will be able to effectively deal with this stressor.

→   When will you start?

Now you have some strategies to counter stress that, if utilized, may assist you in stopping stress before it stops you. Remember, these techniques are ineffective unless you apply them to your everyday life before, during, and after work. I challenge each of you today, regardless of what your occupation is, to make an honest effort to find and commit to at least one technique you feel comfortable using. Practice this technique for two weeks and see if you notice any differences in your attitude, levels of stress, and/or physical well-being. Once you master a skill, add a new one.

"It's better to have it and not need it, than to need it and not have it." This is the advice from Master Lawrence Whitaker of the Urban Defense Center in Philadelphia. He holds a 6th Degree Black Belt in the Mongolian Kempo and Naphtali martial arts systems, among many other impressive credentials. His principle of preparation holds true for physical and emotional challenges. If you are prepared, challenge, pressure, and stress have less of a chance of having a negative impact on you.

Each person determines his or her daily amount of stress, and I'm determined to help you help yourself lower that amount. Something that was personally very helpful to me with managing my stress was that I made it a mission of mine to become an expert on managing stress and performing under pressure with confidence. It was a long road, but I know that control, capability, and connection paved the way.

26

The Crazy and the Lazy

Eliminate the Noise and Be a Solution Starter

nteracting with and working with people who cause more problems than they solve is just part of life. When I work with executives, I often set the tone by asking two simple questions. First I ask, "What are the characteristics of the best boss you have ever worked for?" People come up with characteristics such as: visionary, honest, fair, credible, etc. However, that question isn't what people have the most energy for. Yes, people enjoy the conversation about learning how to be the best possible boss they can be, but it's not as powerful as the second question: "What are the characteristics of the worst boss you have ever worked for?"

This question is a spark for an emotional conversation. People are immediately able to identify that boss who not only wasn't effective, but also actually held them back. Why is it that people are so much more impacted by a bad boss than a good boss? In a couple of words: *social scars.*

Social scars are the experiences that have had a lasting negative impact on us. Earlier in Chapter 7, I walked you through why listening can be bad for your health and how the negative messages we have internalized can limit us. Social scars go beyond limitations. They cut deeper. They are experiences that literally make us avoid people and challenges all because of the fear of having that same experience. Whether it's intentional or not, being in dysfunctional situations consistently can cause us to develop fears and self-defeating behaviors.

One of the first things I tell clients who are going through an executive coaching process is that all people are a little crazy. I tell them this so they realize that leadership is an art based on science and everyone is unique, including themselves. This uniqueness can either be a multiplier of performance or a divider of performance. What I mean by this is that on the financial side of the business, there are clear cause-and-effect options. If your monthly expenses are greater than the amount of cash you have coming in, you have a cash flow problem. If you have a cash flow problem, you have clear options from which to choose. You can cut your monthly expenses, or you can shorten the amount of time clients have to pay bills. As long as you have more money coming in than going out, you are good to go.

With people it's harder to diagnose, and there is not always a clear cause-and-effect relationship. However, once you realize that you aren't going to get it right all of the time, you can start to focus on getting better at reading people and situations so you can make strategic decisions.

Whether you know it or not, we all have a little crazy. This doesn't mean that you are someone who is hearing voices or is out of touch with reality. When you are trained in diagnosing psychological disorders, you learn that there are groups of behaviors that, when present, are considered to have a specific diagnosis. The truth is that all people have tendencies, thoughts, and behaviors that are the same as people who are considered to have mental illness. Often, where the difference lies is in the intensity, duration, and frequency of behaviors as well as how much they impede your daily functioning in life.

An example of this is someone who often has social anxiety and becomes so nervous that it impacts their bodies, such as getting a headache or a stomachache. I don't know anyone who hasn't had some type of physical symptom from being nervous. The point is that we all have certain characteristics that can impede our pathway to success if we let them. The key is to not let your quirks derail your success or the success of others and to not let other people's problems derail you.

Bad bosses or dysfunctional colleagues do more damage than an effective boss or cordial colleague does good. Now I'm not saying that there aren't those amazing bosses or colleagues out there that have tremendous positive impact on your career, but I am saying that the damage that is done by dysfunctional people has greater impact and is seen more often. Dealing with dysfunction isn't just for harmony's sake; there is a clear business case. The more toxic people there are in an organization, the more likely key talent will leave.

Simple Success Strategy: Eliminate the Noise and Be a Solution Starter

Even if it doesn't feel like it, we always have a choice. We have a choice to let other people's issues and challenges bring us down, or we can be strong and keep moving along. There will always be challenges in our lives as well as challenging people. I work with scientists in big pharmaceutical companies. My role is to help them develop practical skills related to effective conversations and leadership. The most common challenge that they present is dealing with difficult people.

The unfortunate aspect of this is that leaders tend to spend an overwhelmingly disproportionate amount of time on the people who are difficult rather than the ones who are high performers. It's not your job to fix everybody, but it is your job to insulate other people from difficult people. That means if you are the boss, you need to address behavior that isn't aligned with what you want early and often. The best predictor of whether people are going to think it is all right to act up is whether or not their superiors let it slide.

It's not your role to be a psychologist and diagnose what is wrong with people. It is your role to try and guide people in the right direction. As the title of this chapter suggests, some difficult people may literally be crazy, whereas others may just be lazy. My advice is not to focus on what's wrong, but to focus on what "right" looks like for you. The shift happens when, rather than only focusing on what people are doing wrong or what you don't want, you also focus on what people can move toward and what they can do.

Eliminate the Noise

In order to eliminate the noise, you first need to know where the noise is coming from. Just as relationships are key to success, relationships are also the key to one's demise. If you are not smart about it, you can often get stuck in surrounding yourself with people who pull you down rather than propel you forward. Now I am not suggesting that you go through your phone book and eliminate people from your life. I am saying that it would be wise to be aware of who you spend your time with and how they impact you. People have a positive, neutral, or negative impact on your success. It's okay if someone is neutral; but if someone has a negative impact on you, it's best to limit your interactions with that person. It doesn't mean that you can never talk to them, but it does mean you probably don't want to seek their advice or be around them when you are working toward your vision.

Be a Solution Starter

The best way to not be derailed by other people is to have a focus of your own. Where people typically go wrong is when they try to change and control others. Practice the mantra: focus on yourself. I really like the title of the book, *People Can't Drive You Crazy If You Don't Give Them the Keys* (Bechtle, 2012). It's a great reminder that we have control of ourselves. This is an attitude and it's contagious. You can set the tone by letting people know that you don't want to hear complaints and comparisons to others. However, you do want people to be competitive with themselves and to compare themselves with themselves. Keep the focus on their development and what they can do to help themselves grow.

Converse with Confidence

Conversations are your greatest tool in dealing with and redirecting behavior. In any given conversation, there are three areas that are critical: the opening, the transition, and the close. You want to be prepared and confident in what you will say and how you will say it in each of these three areas. The way to do that is to have a strategy for each phase of the conversation. The framework, reflect, redirect, and reinforce, will serve as a simple reminder for what to do when. There is an art to conversations and sometimes you will need to reflect and listen longer than usual in order to get to the redirection piece.

In the opening, it is critical to have your headline and be prepared with how you want to set up the conversation. Transitions are a point in the conversation where you want or need to redirect the person. Difficult people are quite effective at derailing conversations. It's your job to refocus the person and the conversation in a clear and kind way. Further on are some examples of transition statements that you can leverage. The idea is to validate what the person is saying and refocus the conversation. The close is where you review what you agreed to and identify the next steps. Clarity is king, so you want to make sure that you have communicated your key messages and that they are understood.

Reflect *(during the opening and into the transition).* Find common ground and send the message that you are confident and want to understand the other person's situation. Summarize and communicate understanding during your opening and throughout the conversation. This includes asking questions and understanding the other person's point of view. The goal is to get the person to feel more comfortable and help them feel secure in your relationship.

Redirect *(during the transition).* Redirect with confidence and kindness. This is where you take the lead and are assertive either through making statements or asking leading questions.

Reinforce *(during the close).* Reinforce what you discussed, decided, and what the next steps are. Ideally, you can give people hope and a plan during the reinforce phase.

There will be times, for example, if it's the third conversation about the same topic, that it would be appropriate to start with reinforce. The reason for this is you are likely moving closer to a performance issue and you need to be clear and candid. Again, you can be clear and kind at the same time.

The following are examples of transition statements. Identify 3–5 that work for you or that you can adapt to fit your style. These statements are helpful to use when someone is pulling you off course in a conversation. The strategy is to reflect and then redirect, which will set you up to reinforce your key messages.

- → I appreciate that insight and . . .
- → That is an important point, let's come back to that . . .
- → I do have suggestions. Let me hear what you think first and then . . .
- → I can see how that would be difficult. May I offer a suggestion?
- → I understand your point of view. It will be beneficial to first focus on . . .
- → How about we look at this from a different perspective?
- → I want to hear your thinking. First I'd like to discuss . . .
- → I am sure you have many examples. However, we are here to focus on working together to increase your effectiveness related to . . .
- → Given that we seem to have different views, let's take two minutes each to talk through the way we each see things.
- → How about after we discuss this topic, you also leverage person X?
- → How does this help us in resolving the situation?
- → I appreciate you sharing your thoughts. Let me share mine, and you can validate with another person.

→ Let's discuss this a little further. I'd like to hear your perspective and then approach this from a business perspective.

→ I hear your concern, and how can you try and improve this situation?

→ I hear your concern with how we have talked about developing this person. How do you see this as an opportunity to develop this person's skill set?

→ I do have some thoughts on this; however, I'd like to hear your thoughts first.

→ I understand that you're not satisfied with your assessment. Let's work on ways to correct the situation and improve performance for year-end.

→ I appreciate that you are disappointed. Let's focus our conversation on what we need to do together.

→ We are not here to focus on person X. Let's focus on you.

→ I hear that you don't see it as an issue. Let me be clear, it is viewed as an issue.

There will always be people who create difficult situations. The key is to minimize the impact of dysfunctional behavior so it doesn't become the norm. First, you need to ensure you aren't someone who is causing challenges. Second, you need to have strategies to insulate yourself from dysfunctional behavior. Finally, if you want to be a leader, you need to help redirect people who are getting in the way of other people's success. People will be much more likely to move toward what you want rather than away from what you want if there is hope and a plan, so focus forward.

CONCLUSION:
YOUR NEXT MOVE

Congratulations. At this point, you have either read every chapter, jumped from chapter to chapter, or just skipped to the end. All three paths have value in their own way. If you read every chapter, now you have a range of simple strategies that you can apply today to set you up for success tomorrow. If you jumped from chapter to chapter and leveraged the "choose your own adventure" approach, you got out of the book what you needed. If you just jumped to the end, then you're looking for the most direct route to success. I can appreciate the jump to the finish.

Initially, I was thinking of calling this book, *Take the Easy Way Out*, because I wanted to focus on all the things that were easy. However, I realized that easy and lazy aren't the answers, but simple and strategic are. As I mentioned earlier in the book, there are differences between a shortcut and a smart-cut. A shortcut in the long run can end up cutting you short. This means you may not learn all you needed to learn to have a strong foundation. What you cut out can come back to bite you. There is always an element of risk in taking a shortcut. I am not saying don't take shortcuts; I am saying be smart about what you cut and anticipate the costs and benefits.

A smart-cut takes into consideration the work that needs to be put in so you can take the most direct route to success. If you just skipped to the end, you will find some value, but you won't find a magical formula to get you to success without putting in some effort. My advice is if you just skipped to the end, go back and pick some topics that interest you and master a few success strategies.

The Power of the View From You

What you see is who you will be. It's that simple. Our beliefs drive our behaviors. If someone expects that they will be great, no matter what their craft, they will have a higher probability of being great. Yes, there will always be obstacles and realities. For example, if a man is 5 feet tall and 100 pounds, it's going to be pretty tough for him to make it in most professional contact sports. At the same time, if that person expects to be great, that grit will serve him well. Even if he doesn't make it as a professional athlete, he can apply that persistence to other parts of his professional and personal life.

The premise for this book was to help you understand what you're made of and to make adjustments to help propel you in the direction that you want. In preparation for the book, I asked Caitlyn McNair, who is a talented and eager student at The College of New Jersey, to review the current research on success. What's unique about Caitlyn is that as much ambition as she has to achieve, it is matched with a desire to volunteer and help people. It's rare to find that combination, and a combination that will serve her well on her path to success. She identified three core factors across the research: self-efficacy (belief in one's ability to achieve a task), persistence, and versatility. Her findings were aligned with the *Simple Is the New Smart* Four Foundations for Success. Self-efficacy and persistence relate to *Psychological Swagger* and versatility is aligned with *Reading* and *Leading*. Although *Accelerating* didn't come up in the review, it is about moving toward success fast.

When I was in graduate school, I lived with a medical student. I had the privilege of learning all about the grueling process of going through med school. I'll never forget the day my buddy, renowned Johns Hopkins Doctor, Eric McCollum, MD, came home after delivering a baby for the first time. I couldn't help but think, "Man, if I was having a baby I wouldn't want some rookie doc delivering." What he explained to me stuck with me, and I think is a great metaphor for development. He said that in medical training, a model they often follow is "See one, Do one, and Teach one." When you learn about something new, you observe and learn how to perform the critical task. Then you perform the task with supervision and get feedback. Then, when you are ready, you teach how to perform the task. It's a cycle of development that provides support and challenge. It helps people grow with a safety net. The reason I mention this metaphor is I think it is a great way to engage in success. Know what you want to accomplish and then find the skills, relationships, and knowledge you need to get there. Along the way as you develop new skills, learn and then teach.

The act and art of helping others help themselves as you progress and succeed leads to positive returns on your investment. One of the best pieces of advice in this book didn't come from one of my simple strategy interviews; it came during a genuine moment in a leadership development session when senior leaders were talking to emerging leaders. Caren Snead Williams, who is the Vice President Deputy General Counsel for JM Family Enterprises, offered what has been most helpful in her career. She started by saying, "Hello, my name is Caren, and I'm a work in progress." Caren has been with JM Family for 20 years and is someone who has a lot of credibility based on her success. She could have just spoken about her accomplishments, but she spoke about her progression. She sent the message that even when you are a senior leader, there is still work that can be done to grow, and not just on the business. Her decision to be real in that moment had a huge positive impact on her colleagues and just as big of an impact on me. It reminded me of the power of being personal, being real, and being focused on progress.

People will always be in pursuit of something. It's the way our minds work. If we know our minds will automatically move toward something, we may as well identify what that something is and set a strategy to get there and fast. In work and life, there are many speed bumps on the journey to success. Don't be one of them. When you fall or fail, fail forward, it will be your intentional step toward success. Your focus is your fuel toward the future you want.

Thank you for taking the time to read and learn with me. Success doesn't have to be about how many hours you spend or how hard you work. Success does have to be about intention and influence. As you progress toward your success, help others help themselves along the way. It may not be easy, but it is simple. Enjoy the journey and bring others along!

BIBLIOGRAPHY

Bechtle, Mike. *People Can't Drive You Crazy If You Don't Give Them the Keys.* Grand Rapids, M.I.: Revell, 2012.

Bridges, William. *Managing Transitions: Making the Most of Change.* New York: Da Capo Press, 2009.

Cialdini, Robert B. *Harnessing the Science of Persuasion.* Boston: Harvard Business Review Press, 2001.

Dye, Renee, and Olivier Sibony. "How to Improve Strategic Planning." *McKinsey Quarterly* Autumn (2007).

Ericsson, K., Ralf Krampe, and Clemens Tesch-Romer. "The Role of Deliberate Practice in the Acquisition of Expert Performance." *Psychological Review* 100 (1993): 363–406.

Fazio, Robert. "Calculating Your Motivational Currency." *OnPoint Advising Blog,* May 15, 2015, http://onpointadvising.com/calculating-motivational-currency/.

———. "Emotional Intelligence in Action." *OnPoint Advising Blog,* July 30, 2015, http://onpointadvising.com/emotional-intelligence-in-action/.

Fazio, R.J., L.M. Fazio, and Editors. *Finding Your Way Through Sudden Loss and Adversity*. Closter, N.J.: Hold The Door For Others, 2006.

Gladwell, Malcolm. *Blink: The Power of Thinking Without Thinking*. New York: Back Bay Books, 2007.

Kouzes, James, and Barry Posner. *Credibility: How Leaders Gain and Lose It, Why People Demand It*. Flushing, N.Y.: Gildan Media, 2003.

Mayer, J.D., and P. Salovey. *What is Emotional Intelligence?* New York: Basic Books, 1997.

McClelland, David C. *The Achieving Society*. Princeton, N.J.: D. Van Nostrand Company, Inc., 1961.

Nussbaum, J. *The Handbook of Lifespan Communication*. New York: Peter Lang Publishing, 2014.

Pham, Lien B., and Shelley E. Taylor. "From Thought to Action: Effects of Process-Versus Outcome-Based Mental Simulations on Performance." *Personality and Social Psychology Bulletin* 25 (1999): 250–260.

Reichheld, Fred, and Rob Markey. *The Ultimate Question 2.0 (Revised and Expanded Edition): How Net Promoter Companies Thrive in a Customer-Driven World*. Boston: Harvard Business Review Press, 2011.

Seligman, Martin E., and Steven F. Maier. "Failure to Escape Traumatic Shock." *Journal of Experimental Psychology* 74 (1967): 1–9.

"The Social-Ecological Model: A Framework for Prevention." Center for Disease Control and Prevention. Accessed June 2015, http://www.cdc.gov /violenceprevention/overview/social-ecological model.html.

Sternberg, Robert. *Successful Intelligence: How Practical and Creative Intelligence Determine Success in Life.* East Rutherford, N.J.: Plume, 1997.

Van Boven, Leaf, and Thomas Gilovich. "To Do or to Have: That is the Question." *Journal of Personality and Social Psychology* 85 (2003): 1193–1202.

INDEX

ABOUT THE AUTHOR

Rob Fazio, PhD, simplifies success so you can move forward fast. An executive adviser, sport psychologist, crisis consultant, keynote speaker, and nonprofit leader, Dr. Fazio partners with senior executives and athletes to remove roadblocks and get results. He has worked with Fortune 500 companies around the globe for more than 15 years. He is the Managing Partner of OnPoint Advising, Inc., and President of the nonprofit Hold the Door for Others. He is often sought out to share his point of view on CNN, Fox News Channel, and MSNBC. His straightforward approach, balanced with wisdom and humor, is what his clients find useful and refreshing. His passion is connecting people and businesses to their confidence so they can find simple strategies to succeed.